Why Does Inequality Matter?

UEHIRO SERIES IN PRACTICAL ETHICS

General Editor: Julian Savulescu, University of Oxford

Choosing Children
The Ethical Dilemmas of Genetic Intervention
Jonathan Glover

Messy Morality
The Challenge of Politics
C. A. J. Coady

Killing in War
Jeff McMahan

Beyond Humanity?
The Ethics of Biomedical Enhancement
Allen Buchanan

Ethics for Enemies
Terror, Torture, and War
F. M. Kamm

Unfit for the Future
The Need for Moral Enhancement
Ingmar Persson and Julian Savulescu

The Robust Demands of the Good
Ethics with Attachment, Virtue, and Respect
Philip Pettit

Why Does Inequality Matter?
T. M. Scanlon

Why Does Inequality Matter?

T. M. Scanlon

OXFORD
UNIVERSITY PRESS

OXFORD

UNIVERSITY PRESS

Great Clarendon Street, Oxford, OX2 6DP,
United Kingdom

Oxford University Press is a department of the University of Oxford.
It furthers the University's objective of excellence in research, scholarship,
and education by publishing worldwide. Oxford is a registered trade mark of
Oxford University Press in the UK and in certain other countries

© T. M. Scanlon 2018

The moral rights of the author have been asserted

First Edition published in 2018

Impression: 7

Published in the United States of America by Oxford University Press
198 Madison Avenue, New York, NY 10016, United States of America

British Library Cataloguing in Publication Data
Data available

Library of Congress Control Number: 2017943303

ISBN 978-0-19-881269-2

Printed in Great Britain by
CPI Group (UK) Ltd, Croydon CR0 4YY

For Jessie and Sarah

Contents

Preface

This book is a revised and extended version of my Uehiro Lectures, given in Oxford in December 2013. I am grateful to Julian Savulescu and the Uehiro Foundation for the invitation to give those lectures, and grateful to John Broome, David Miller, and Janet Radcliffe Richards, my commentators on that occasion, for their thoughtful remarks.

The ideas presented here go back to my 1996 Lindley Lecture, "The Diversity of Objections to Inequality." That lecture developed into a paper called "When Does Equality Matter?" ever-longer versions of which were presented to more audiences than I can list. I benefitted greatly from the many comments and suggestions that I received on all of those occasions. The invitation to give the Uehiro Lectures provided a very welcome stimulus to extend that unfinished paper into three lectures, which now have grown to ten chapters.

Many people have given me valuable help at various stages of this process of development. Charles Beitz, Joshua Cohen, Joseph Fishkin, Samuel Freeman, Niko Kolodny, Martin O'Neill, Joseph Raz, Amartya Sen, Tommie Shelby, Dennis Thompson, Manuel Vargas, and Paul Weithman gave me helpful comments on draft chapters, and in some cases even on full drafts of the book. I also received incisive and instructive comments from the participants in my political philosophy seminar in the spring term of 2016, including especially Frances Kamm and Jed Lewinsohn. My heartfelt thanks to all of these people. It is wonderful to have such generous and helpful friends and colleagues. I also thank Richard de Filippi for discussion of inequality in access to health care and in health outcomes, and Noel Dominguez for research assistance.

As always, I am grateful to my wife, Lucy, for her support, and for responding thoughtfully and patiently to my repeated attempts, over dinners and breakfasts, to explain why I was finding inequality such a difficult topic to write about.

1

Introduction

The extremely high levels of inequality now prevailing in the United States and in the world as a whole are open to serious moral objection. But it is not clear exactly why this is so—not clear what the moral reasons are for objecting to inequality and for reducing or eliminating it if possible. Gaining a better understanding of these reasons is the aim of this book.

One reason for wanting to redistribute resources from the rich to the poor is simply that this is a way of making the poor better off, at comparatively small cost to the welfare of the rich. This can be a strong reason for supporting redistributive policies, but it is not, at base, an objection to *inequality*, that is to say, an objection to the difference between the well-being of some and that of others. It is simply a reason, perhaps very powerful, for increasing the well-being of the poor. The fact that some people are much better off than the poor is relevant to this rationale for redistribution only because, as Willie Sutton, a famous American bank robber, is said to have remarked when asked why he robbed banks: "That's where the money is."

Egalitarian reasons, by contrast, are reasons for objecting to the difference between what some have and what others have, and for reducing this difference. In what follows, I will be particularly concerned with reasons of this kind, not because they are more important than reasons for improving the lot of those who are worse off—often they are not more important—but because they are more puzzling.

Concern with equality can seem difficult to justify. Robert Nozick, for example, famously charged that a concern with equality is a concern with a particular pattern of distribution, which can be maintained only by interfering with the liberty of individuals to make choices, take risks, and enter into contracts that would upset that pattern.[1] Why, he asked,

---

[1] *Anarchy, State, and Utopia*, 160–4. (Works will be cited in footnotes only by title. Full publication information can be found in the bibliography.)

should we try to maintain an arbitrary pattern of distribution at the cost of constant interference with individual liberty?

When the idea that there is a conflict between equality and liberty is put in this abstract way, equality seems immediately at a disadvantage. Interference with liberty is something people have obvious reason to object to: no one wants to be deprived of options that he or she values, or to be told what to do by others. But it is less clear what reasons there are for objecting to inequality. People have good reason to wish that their own lives were better. But what reason do they have to be concerned with the difference between their lives and the lives of others? It has thus often been charged that demands for greater equality are just expressions of envy that the "have nots" feel toward the "haves."

Reasons can be egalitarian—concerned with equality and inequality— in either a broader or a narrower sense. Reasons are egalitarian in the broader sense as long as they are reasons for objecting to the difference between what some have and what others have. This includes reasons that are based on the consequences of this difference, even when the reasons for objecting to these consequences have nothing to do with equality. There is, for example, considerable empirical evidence that inequality has very serious effects on the health of those who have less.[2] This provides strong instrumental reasons for reducing inequality that are egalitarian in the broad, but not the narrow sense, since reasons for concern with ill-health are not themselves egalitarian. Reasons are egalitarian in the narrower sense if they are grounded, ultimately, in some idea of why equality itself is to be sought, or why inequality itself is objectionable. One possible reason for objecting to economic inequality is that it can give those who have more an unacceptable degree of control over the lives of those who have less. If the reason for finding this control unacceptable is the unequal relationship between the dominated and those dominating them, then this objection is egalitarian in the narrow as well as the broader sense. If, on the other hand, the objection to being controlled is just the loss of opportunities that it involves, then the objection is egalitarian only in the broader sense.

---

[2] See Michael Marmot, *Status Syndrome: How your Social Standing Directly Affects Your Health*, and Richard Wilkinson and Kate Pickett, *The Spirit Level: Why More Equal Societies Almost Always Do Better*. For discussion, see Martin O'Neill, "The Facts of Inequality."

Nozick's charge, that a concern with equality is a concern to preserve a certain pattern of distribution, is framed as a challenge primarily to reasons that are egalitarian in the narrower sense. But the envy objection questions whether there are any good reasons *at all* for objecting to inequality, whether these reasons are narrowly egalitarian or not.

Insofar as a reason for reducing inequality is even broadly egalitarian—insofar as it is a reason for objecting to the *difference* between what some have and what others have—it might seem to count in favor of reducing that difference even if this made no one better off, and left at least some people (the rich) worse off. The apparent irrationality of such a move is the basis of what has been called the "leveling down objection." This objection has been offered as a reason for rejecting egalitarianism in favor of *prioritarianism*, the view that we should be concerned simply with improving the condition of the worse off rather than with the difference between rich and poor.[3]

To assess these challenges we need a clear account of the reasons for caring about equality and inequality. We also need such an account in order to understand what is wrong with laws and institutions that promote inequality, and how changing these institutions to bring about greater equality can be justified. Even if it would be a very good thing if the poor were better off, or a good thing if the difference between the poor and the rich were reduced, it might still be the case that achieving these aims by redistribution would be wrong. Willie Sutton was, after all, a robber, and the same could be said for Robin Hood, even though his motives were better.

I believe that there are reasons for objecting to inequality that meet these challenges—indeed, that there are a number of diverse reasons. The task of this book is to investigate the nature of these reasons. I describe this task as investigating the objections to inequality rather than the case

---

[3] See Derek Parfit, "Equality or Priority?" and Harry Frankfurt, "Equality as a Moral Ideal," and *On Inequality*. For discussion of the issue, see Martin O'Neill, "What Should Egalitarians Believe." Frankfurt's central thesis is that we should be concerned with "sufficiency"—whether everyone has *enough* for a good life—rather than with equality—the difference between what some have and what others have (*On Inequality*, 7 et passim). He acknowledges, however, that there can be good "derivative" reasons for objecting to inequality that are not based on the moral value of equality (*On Inequality*, 9, 16–17). He goes on to mention many of the reasons for objecting to inequality that I will discuss later in this book. So I take it that Frankfurt is objecting only to reasons that are egalitarian in the narrower sense that I distinguished.

for equality because this way of putting it includes, potentially, a wider range of considerations, not all of which are egalitarian in the narrower sense. As we will see, some of the most powerful objections to inequality have to do with its consequences, and not all of these objections are based in the value of equality.

Recognizing the diversity of the reasons for objecting to inequality is important also because it helps us to understand the differences between the kinds of inequality that we face. The inequality between the 1 percent and the rest of us is one thing; the inequality between the comfortably well-off and the very poor is something else. Racial inequality, and the various forms of inequality between men and women, are yet different problems, as is inequality between people in different countries. These different forms of inequality are subject to different combinations of moral objections of the kinds I will describe.

One important idea of equality that I will presuppose but not argue for is what might be called basic moral equality—the idea that everyone counts morally, regardless of differences such as their race, their gender, and where they live. The increased acceptance of the idea of basic moral equality, and the expansion of the range of people it is acknowledged to cover, has been perhaps the most important form of moral progress over the centuries.

Basic moral equality is now widely accepted, even among people who reject more substantive egalitarian claims. Nozick, for example, accepts basic moral equality. When he writes, "Individuals have rights," he means *all* individuals.[4] But he denies that we owe it to people, morally speaking, to make their condition equal to that of others in wealth, income, or any other particular respect. It is substantive equality of the latter kinds that I will be concerned with in this book. My question is: when and why is it morally objectionable that some people are worse off in some way than others are? In the remainder of this chapter I will identify several kinds of reasons for objecting to inequality, many of which will be examined in more detail in later chapters.

Status: Caste systems and other social arrangements that involve stigmatizing differences in status are leading historical examples of objectionable inequality. In these systems, members of some groups are

---

[4] *Anarchy, State, and Utopia*, ix.

regarded as inferior. They are excluded from social roles and occupations that are seen as most desirable, or even relegated to occupations that are regarded as demeaning and beneath the dignity of members of other groups. The evil involved in such arrangements has a comparative character: what is objectionable is being treated as *inferior to others* in a demeaning way. The root idea of the objection to this is thus an egalitarian one.

In the historical cases of the kind I have mentioned, inequalities based on caste, race, or gender were a matter of law or of entrenched social customs and attitudes. In some cases these attitudes involved widely shared beliefs that members of some races do not have full moral status, perhaps even that they are "not fully human," thus denying what I just called basic moral equality. But such beliefs are not essential to the objection I am concerned with. The class system in nineteenth-century Britain did not, I assume, involve the idea that members of the lower classes were not fully human, or that what happened to them did not matter morally, but only that they were not suited for, or entitled to, certain social and political roles.

Economic inequality can also be objectionable for the reason I am now discussing, because extreme inequality in income and wealth can mean that the poor must live in a way that is reasonably seen as humiliating. As Adam Smith observed, it is a serious objection to a society if some people are so much poorer than others that they have to live and dress in such a way that they cannot go out in public without shame.[5] The evil here is, again, comparative—it is not merely having ragged clothes, or poor housing, but of having to live and to present oneself in a way that is so far below the standard generally accepted in the society that it marks one as inferior. As this reference to "standards generally accepted" indicates, economic inequalities have these effects only given certain prevailing attitudes about what it necessary in order for someone to be socially acceptable. So what is objectionable is a certain combination of economic inequality and social norms. I will discuss this kind of inequality further in Chapter 3.

Control: Inequalities can also be objectionable because they give some people an unacceptable degree of control over the lives of others. If, for

---

[5] *An Inquiry into the Nature and Causes of the Wealth of Nations*, 351–2. Cited by Amartya Sen in *Inequality Reexamined*, 115.

example, a small number of people control almost all of the wealth in a society, this can give them an unacceptable degree of control over where and how others can work, what is available for them to buy, and in general what their lives will be like. More narrowly, ownership of important public media in a country can give some an objectionable degree of control over how others in the society view themselves and their lives, and how they understand their society. I will discuss objections to these two forms of control in Chapters 6, 7, and 9.[6]

Equality of Opportunity: When there is great inequality in family income and wealth, individuals' prospects of success in a competitive market are greatly affected by the families into which they are born. This can make it difficult or impossible to achieve equality of economic opportunity. This is widely recognized as a serious problem, although the case for equality of opportunity is not much discussed. I will examine that case, and its implications for inequality, in Chapters 4 and 5.

Political Fairness: Great inequalities in wealth and income can also undermine the fairness of political institutions. The wealthy may be much more able than others to influence the course of political discussion, more able to gain political office themselves, and more able to influence others who hold office. This can be seen as a special case of the problem of control: manipulation of the political system is one way of turning economic advantage into control. But undermining the fairness of the political system is morally significant in other ways, for example, because it affects the legitimacy of laws and policies. I will discuss this objection to inequality, and the degree to which it is a matter of unequal influence, or unequal opportunity to influence, in Chapter 6.

Objections of the four kinds that I have listed make it clear how some objections to economic inequality are not mere expressions of envy. They also make clear that what these objections call for is not pointless leveling down. People have good reason to object to stigmatizing differences in status, to objectionable forms of control, and to social institutions that

---

[6] Marmot and others argue that the effects of inequality on health seem mainly to be brought about through the two effects of inequality that I have just listed: the experience of having low social status and of being under the control of others, particularly in the workplace. See Michael Marmot et al., "Employment Grade and Coronary Heart Disease in British Civil Servants," and other works I cited in n. 2. This is questioned by Angus Deaton, "What does the Empirical Evidence Tell us about the Injustice of Health Inequalities?", 270–2.

are unfair, even if eliminating these things would not increase their welfare. Fair political institutions and equal economic opportunity may lead to the poor being better off. But this is not the only reason for wanting institutions that are fair. The poor have reason to want equality of opportunity—to want to be treated fairly—even if it does not in the end lead to their being better off. (It is a further question whether the poor would have *sufficient* reason to want equality of opportunity if this meant that they would be less well off economically.)

Equal Concern: Some other objections to inequality are not, like the ones I have just listed, based on its effects, but rather on the ways in which this inequality arises. Objections based on the idea of equal concern are of this kind. These objections apply when an institution or agent owes some benefit to every member of a certain group but provides this benefit only to some, or more fully to some than to others.

Suppose, for example, that a municipality is obligated to provide paved streets and sanitation to all residents. It would then be objectionable, absent some special justification, to provide these services at a higher level to some than to others. For example, it would be objectionable for the town to repave the streets more frequently in rich neighborhoods than poor ones, or more frequently in the areas where friends of the mayor or members of a certain religious group live. This requirement of equal concern is not violated every time the municipal government spends more money to provide a certain service for some than it does for others. If, for example, geological factors made it more difficult to maintain passable roads in some areas than in others, spending more to maintain roads in these areas would not be objectionable in this way, because the justification for doing this does not require giving the interests of residents of this area greater weight than the comparable interests of residents of other areas.[7] I will discuss this requirement in Chapter 3, considering how it should be understood and in what sense it is based on an idea of equality.

Fair Distribution of Income: In 1965 the average compensation of executives in the 350 largest firms in the U.S. was twenty times the average compensation of workers in those firms. In the last decades of the twentieth century, this ratio grew rapidly, and reached a high of 376

---

[7] I call this a requirement of equal concern rather than equal treatment because it applies not to the benefits provided but to the way in which these benefits can be justified.

to 1 in 2000. In 2014 it was still 303 to 1, "higher than it had been at any time during the 1960s, 1970s, 1980s or 1990s."[8] In addition, "From 1978 to 2014, inflation adjusted compensation [of these executives] increased 997 percent, a rise almost double stock market growth and substantially greater than the painfully slow 10.5 percent growth in a typical worker's annual compensation over the same period."[9]

This inequality seems clearly objectionable. What is objectionable about it is not that it represents a failure of equal concern. The benefits in question are not ones that some agent is obligated to provide and is providing unequally. Rather, the benefits are ones that individuals obtain by participating in the economy in one way or another. The objection might be put by saying that these figures indicate that the economic institutions that give rise to this inequality are unfair. One way in which such institutions could be unfair would be a lack of equality of opportunity, which I have already mentioned and will discuss more fully in Chapters 4 and 5. The present objection is different, however. What is held to be unfair is the way in which unequal rewards are assigned to certain economic roles or positions rather than the lack of opportunity that individuals have to compete for those positions. This raises the question of what fairness of this kind requires. I will discuss this question in Chapter 9.

To summarize the discussion so far: I have identified six kinds of reasons for objecting to various forms of inequality and for seeking to eliminate or reduce them:

(1) Inequality can be objectionable because it creates humiliating differences in status.

(2) Inequality can be objectionable because it gives the rich unacceptable forms of power over those who have less.

(3) Inequality can be objectionable because it undermines equality of economic opportunity.

(4) Inequality can be objectionable because it undermines the fairness of political institutions.

---

[8] Lawrence Mishel and Alyssa Davis, "Top CEOs Make 300 Times More than Typical Workers," 2.

[9] Mishel and Davis, "Top CEOs," 1–2.

(5) Inequality can be objectionable because it results from violation of a requirement of equal concern for the interests of those to whom the government is obligated to provide some benefit.

(6) Inequality of income and wealth can be objectionable because it arises from economic institutions that are unfair.

In contrast to luck egalitarian views, which take (non-voluntary) inequality to be bad wherever it occurs,[10] the objections to inequality that I have listed all presuppose some form of relationship or interaction between the unequal parties. Objectionable inequalities in status presuppose some relationship that makes feelings of humiliation or diminished self-esteem reasonable. Such objections thus do not apply to people who have no interaction with one another. Objections based on control apply only where inequalities involve or lead to some form of control. Objections based on failures of equal concern presuppose some agent or agency that is obligated to provide benefits of the kind in question, and objections based on interference with economic opportunity, interference with political equality, or unfair distribution of income all presuppose that the parties participate in or are subject to some institution to which requirements of fairness apply. Once inequality is considered separately from all such relational and institutional factors, it is not clear that it is objectionable.[11]

The fact that many of these reasons for objecting to inequality apply only where there are institutions with certain obligations, or institutions to which certain requirements of justice apply, may lead readers to identify my position with what Thomas Nagel calls "the political conception of justice," which holds that justice applies only within the boundaries of a nation state.[12] But my claims differ from this conception in important respects. Not all of the reasons for objecting to inequality

---

[10] See e.g. G. A. Cohen, "On the Currency of Egalitarian Justice," and Richard Arneson, "Equality and Equal Opportunity for Welfare." This is an instance of what Parfit, in "Equality or Priority?," calls Telic Egalitarianism. The term "luck egalitarianism" was coined by Elizabeth Anderson, a critic of the view, in "What is the Point of Equality?" The view of equality that Anderson favors is, like mine, relational (see her p. 313 et passim). For critical discussion, see Samuel Scheffler, "What is Egalitarianism?"

[11] In particular, G. A. Cohen's objections to inequality in *Why Not Socialism?* depend heavily on the particular personal relationships involved in his camping trip example.

[12] "The Problem of Global Justice." For critical discussion of this conception see Joshua Cohen and Charles Sabel, "Extra Rempublicam Nulla Justitia?," and A. J. Julius, "Nagel's Atlas."

that I describe presuppose shared institutions, and where institutions are involved, these institutions need not be coextensive with or enforced by a state. Economic institutions of the kind I discuss in Chapter 8, for example, are not limited by national borders.

There may be other reasons for favoring equality, or for objecting to inequality, that I have not listed. I will focus on the objections I have listed because they seem to me important, but especially because there are interesting normative questions about the values that underlie them. Not all objections to inequality raise such questions. For example, as I mentioned earlier, inequality may be objectionable because it causes ill-health.[13] It might also be argued that greater equality is desirable because inequality leads to social instability, or because equality contributes to economic efficiency by fostering a greater sense of solidarity and willingness to work hard for the common good. If the empirical assumptions underlying such claims are correct, then these are good reasons for regarding inequality as a bad thing. I am not discussing these reasons, however, because there seems to me nothing puzzling about the values that they appeal to. There is no question, for example, about whether ill-health is bad. So the questions of whether these objections apply are purely empirical.

It may be maintained, of course, that the great inequality in current societies is not objectionable at all, because it arises from the legitimate exercise of individual liberties, and that measures intended to reduce this inequality would be objectionable interferences with these liberties. In Chapter 7, I will discuss this objection and examine the ideas of liberty on which it may be based. Another possible justification for economic inequality is that the individuals who have more deserve their greater rewards. I will examine the idea of desert in Chapter 8, and consider whether it can be appealed to as a justification for economic inequality or perhaps as an objection to it.

In Chapter 9, I will examine the idea of unfairness on which the last of the objections I have mentioned is based, and consider how this objection, and others I have discussed, apply to the recent rise in inequality in the United States and other developed countries. Chapter 10 will be a summary of the main themes of the book.

---

[13] See the works cited in n. 2.

2

Equal Concern

In Chapter 1, I listed violations of equal concern as one form of objectionable inequality. As examples, I mentioned cases in which a municipal government provides a much lower a level of public services, such as road paving, sanitation, or public transportation, for some citizens than it provides for others, who may be favored because of their political or religious views, for example, or because they are friends of important public officials.

Objections to inequality of this kind presuppose an obligation on the part of some agent to provide benefits to everyone in a certain group. (Exactly what kind of obligation is presupposed will be a matter for further discussion.) These objections therefore apply only to inequalities that result from the failure of that agent to fulfill this obligation to all those to whom it is owed.

Consider, for example, the following facts. In the U.S., life expectancy for men is 74.2 years; in China, it is 70.4 years; but in Malawi, it is only 37.1 years. This is appalling, and cries out for some action. That is to say, the last fact, about life expectancy in Malawi, is appalling and cries out for action. It is often suggested that the problem is one of inequality, sometimes called "the international life expectancy gap." But although these facts are very troubling, I am not convinced that inequality is what is objectionable in this case.

It is a very bad thing that life expectancy in Malawi is so low. But what is the relevance of the fact that life expectancy is much higher in China and in the United States? This difference might be relevant simply because it indicates that human beings do not have to die so young. Given presently available technology, humans can live much longer, and do live longer under more favorable conditions. So one reason that the low life expectancy of men in Malawi is appalling is that it is avoidable. But referring to this situation as "the international life expectancy gap" suggests that the great *difference* in life expectancy between the three countries itself has fundamental moral significance, and it is not clear to me that it has this significance. It seems to me that what matters is just the low life expectancy in Malawi, not the difference between it and life expectancy in other countries.

Consider by contrast these facts about regional and racial disparity in life expectancy in the United States. In the 10 percent of counties in the U.S. with greatest life expectancy 77 percent of white men live to age 70, while only 68 percent of black men born in those counties live to that age. In the 10 percent of counties with lowest life expectancy things are even worse. 61 percent of white men born in those counties live to age 70 but only 45 percent of black men.[1] According to a 2013 report of the Center for Disease Control and Prevention, there were 1.2 cases of tuberculosis per 100,000 among whites in the U.S. but 10.2 cases per 100,000 among blacks. And the infant mortality rate was 5.8 percent among whites but 13.7 percent among blacks.[2] These figures may be due in part to poverty, but they also raise questions of equality—specifically questions of equal concern—insofar as the differences are due to the fact that public institutions fulfill the obligation of providing medical care and other conditions of public health more fully with respect to whites, and to people living in certain areas, than with respect to blacks, and to people living in other areas. A more general attitude of racial discrimination plays an important role in explaining this disparity in medical treatment, just as unequal treatment in the other cases I mentioned may be explained by particular forms of favoritism. But unequal concern of the kind that the cases have in common is morally objectionable however it may be explained.

To say that what is objectionable about international differences in life expectancy is not the inequality involved (or at least that this inequality is not objectionable for the same kind of reason as racial disparity in life expectancy within the United States) is not to say that these international differences may not raise questions of justice. If low life expectancy in Malawi, say, were due to poverty that resulted from the theft of natural resources by colonial powers, then it would be the result of injustice, not

[1] Mark R. Cullen, Clint Cummins, and Victor R. Fuchs, "Geographic and Racial Variation in Premature Mortality in the U.S.: Analyzing the Disparities." The figures cited are from 1999–2001 mortality rates.

[2] CDC, *Health Disparities and Inequalities Report—United States*, 2013.

simply an unfortunate situation, like the results of a drought or tsunami, that others have humanitarian reasons to help alleviate. But the underlying objection would still not be a matter of inequality. If I have less money than you do because hackers stole the money in my bank account, this is wrong, but not because of the inequality involved. If the poverty that leads to low life expectancy in third world countries is due not only to past colonial practices but to present unjust institutions of international trade, ideas of equality may have a role in explaining why these institutions are unjust. But this is not the question of equality that seems to be implicated by the facts about life expectancy themselves. My point is that the facts about racial disparity in life expectancy in the United States raise a distinct question of equality that does not seem to be involved in the international case, which raises serious moral questions of a different sort.

What is objectionable about international differences in life expectancy would not be made less serious if life expectancy in the U.S. were to be reduced by the occurrence of some new disease, thereby reducing the inequality involved. But this fact does not show that the objection to international differences in life expectancy is not based on the inequality involved. The racial disparity in health conditions in the U.S. would also not be made less objectionable if life expectancy for white males in the U.S. were to decrease for such a reason. This is because what is objectionable about this disparity is not the bare fact of inequality but the factor that causes it, namely a violation of a requirement of equal concern.

This illustrates a general point about the relational view of equality and inequality that I am defending, which I described in Chapter 1. The bare fact of inequality in life expectancy is not what is objectionable in either the international or the domestic case. What is objectionable in both cases is, most basically, that some people's lives are much shorter than they could be, given existing knowledge and technology. Inequality is relevant only insofar as it figures in what is objectionable about the institutions or other factors that produce these differences. The difference between the international and the domestic cases is that in the domestic case, but not the international case, the difference in life expectancy is due the failure of important institutions to meet a requirement of equal concern.[3] If this objectionable inequality were to be

---

[3] A requirement of equal concern can be understood to mean a number of different things. Ronald Dworkin, for example, understands it as the requirement that a

reduced, then *one* objection to the present situation would also be lessened, even if this involved reducing the level of medical care available to whites and did not improve the life expectancy of blacks.[4] Whether this would be justifiable overall is a further question.

The aim of this chapter is to examine this requirement of equal concern in more detail, and in particular to understand the idea of equality that it involves. If the obligation that an institution has toward its citizens is just to treat them in a certain way—for example, not to violate their Nozickean rights—then even if this obligation is owed to all citizens equally, the idea of equality would have no role in explaining the wrong involved when this obligation is fulfilled for some but not for others. The way some people are treated in such a case is wrong because it violates their rights, and this would be wrong in the same way whether the rights of others were being violated or not. The citizens have "equal rights" (that is to say, the *same* rights). But the idea of equality plays no role in explaining why violations of these rights are wrongful.

Some have claimed that the idea of equality, or at least the idea of equality that I am calling equal concern, is empty because the wrongfulness of what may appear to be violations of this requirement can always be explained in this way as a violation of some underlying non-comparative right.[5] But equality does, I believe, play a more significant role in explaining the wrong of unequal concern in some cases.

Consider the question of unequal funding for basic education. Every state constitution in the United States includes some requirement that

government's laws and policies must be justified in a way that treats every citizen as equally important. (See *Sovereign Virtue*, 6.) I accept this requirement, which provides a framework within which all of the objections to inequality that I will discuss can be understood. But I will use the term 'equal concern' to identify one specific way in which this requirement can be violated, namely the unequal fulfillment of an obligation to provide certain benefits. Not all of the objections to inequality I will discuss depend on obligations of this kind. The general idea of equal concern that Dworkin starts from leads to objections to unequal outcomes in one way when we are concerned, as in this chapter, with government's obligations to provide benefits and in a different way when, as in Chapter 9, we are concerned with justifying a system of economic cooperation.

[4] I am grateful to James Brandt for pressing this point in discussion.

[5] See Peter Westen, "The Empty Idea of Equality." Although the title of his article refers to "equality," Westen, writing as a constitutional lawyer, is mainly concerned with the particular idea of equal treatment, which I am calling equal concern. For more general discussion of the question of comparative vs. non-comparative wrongs, see Joel Feinberg, "Non-Comparative Justice."

the state provide basic education for all children. The New Jersey constitution, for example, states that "The Legislature shall provide for the maintenance and support of a thorough and efficient system of free public schools for the instruction of all children in the state between the ages of five and eighteen years."[6] The New Jersey Supreme Court has held that this requirement "must be understood to embrace that educational opportunity which is needed in the contemporary setting to equip a child for his role as a citizen and as a competitor in the labor market."[7] If the state failed to provide education up to this level for some children, this would be a violation of a specific non-comparative requirement, and this has been the case in New Jersey for many years, leading to a long series of cases before the New Jersey Supreme Court.[8] It would be no violation of *this* requirement if the state provided all children with education up to this level but some children had access to additional education, provided by their parents or through private schools. But it would violate a requirement of equal concern if the state itself were to provide education above this minimum level for some children but not for all.[9] It might seem that the plausibility of this comparative objection depends on the fact that education is a competitive good. If some students in a state receive a higher level of education this will place others at a disadvantage "as competitors in the labor market." But I believe that the comparative objection to this kind of unequal treatment does not depend on this competitive element.

To see this, consider a different example, procedural safeguards against wrongful conviction. One way that a legal system can be unjust is by providing inadequate safeguards of this kind. The U.S. legal system is unjust in this non-comparative way because poor and especially black defendants have insufficient protection against being wrongly convicted

---

[6] New Jersey Constitution, Article VIII, Section IV.

[7] *Robinson v. Cahill* 62 N.J. at 515.

[8] For an overview of the controversy in New Jersey, see "School Funding Cases in New Jersey," <http://schoolfundinginfo/2015/01/school-funding-cases-in-new-jersey>. Regarding similar controversy in Kansas, see "School Finding Cases in Kansas," <http://schoolfunding.info/2015/01/school-funding-cases-in-kansas-2>.

[9] Whether a system of school funding that allowed richer school districts to provide a higher level of education would violate the requirement of equal concern would depend on whether this system of funding as a whole is seen as a state policy, through which the state fulfills its obligation to provide schooling, or whether, instead, the municipalities that provide better schooling were seen as separate agents, like private groups of parents.

of crimes. They often have inadequate legal representation, and are frequently pressured into plea bargains that they should not accept.

Any set of procedural safeguards will be imperfect, and could be improved on. But I assume that there is a level of protection, short of perfection, such that a legal system that provides this level of protection for everyone is not open to a charge of non-comparative procedural injustice of this kind. If, however, such a system provided an even higher level of procedural protection for some citizens than for others—if, for example, criminal charges against members of a certain social class, or of a certain religion, had to be supported by a higher standard of proof—this would, absent some special justification, be unjust in a *comparative* sense. Such a legal system would not be providing "equal justice under law," even if no non-comparative right were being violated.

This same analysis applies to the examples I mentioned earlier of unequal provision of public services such as medical care, street paving, or schooling. Perhaps there is a minimum level of these services that the government has a (non-comparative) obligation to provide for all. But whether this is so or not, providing unequal levels of these services to different groups, without some special justification, violates a general (comparative) requirement of equal concern. In many such cases, these differences in treatment may be explained by a background of racial prejudice and discrimination, which is morally objectionable in itself. But inadequate, or unequal, levels of provision can be wrong on non-comparative or comparative grounds that are independent of this objectionable background condition. There are thus three kinds of wrong potentially involved in these cases: a non-comparative wrong of inadequate provision of some benefit, a comparative wrong of unequal concern, and a wrong of racial discrimination.

These distinct wrongs can sometimes be difficult to disentangle. Consider the case of racial profiling, as in the practice of requiring less evidence of likely criminal activity to justify stopping and searching the cars of black motorists than is required to justify stopping and searching the cars of white motorists. This clearly violates a comparative requirement of equal concern. But it may at the same time be a non-comparative wrong. If the level of evidence that the policy requires to justify stopping white motorists provides the minimum level of protection that people are entitled to have against being interfered with in this way, then allowing black motorists to be stopped on the basis of less evidence of possible wrongdoing is a non-comparative wrong as well as an objectionable form of unequal treatment. A general background of racial discrimination may explain both of these comparative and non-comparative wrongs, but they are more general types of wrongs that are independent of this particular cause.

The comparative requirement of equal concern is not violated simply by the fact that a government devotes more resources to providing a given benefit to some than to others. If geological factors make it much more difficult to maintain passable roads in some areas than in others, then spending more on the roads in these areas need not reflect unequal concern for those who live there and those who live in other parts of town. Similarly, it is not a violation of equal concern if a municipality spends more money per pupil on special education classes than on classes for students who are not disabled, because this does not indicate that the interests of children with special needs are being given greater weight than the interests of other children.

In the cases I have considered so far, such as public health, paved streets, education, and protection against wrongful conviction, it is plausible to assume that governments have a specific obligation to provide these benefits, at least up to a certain level, and as long as the cost is not excessive. But the requirement of equal concern can also apply to institutions that have a general obligation to supply benefits to a certain group of individuals even in cases in which there is no obligation to provide a specific good. There are some benefits that governments can choose whether or not to provide. Public swimming pools, ice skating rinks, and golf courses might be examples. But if a government provides benefits of this kind it cannot make them legally available to only some citizens, and, I would say, it can be open to objection if it provides these facilities in a way that is accessible only to people in some neighborhoods.

This does not mean that everything that governments do must benefit all citizens equally. There may be a need for governmental facilities of a certain kind, such as administrative buildings or military establishments. In addition to the benefit that these facilities provide to all, by serving their general public purpose, they may provide additional benefits, such as increased employment opportunities, for those who live in the places in which they are located. This is not, in itself, a violation of the requirement of equal concern that I am describing, because (in contrast to the other cases I have mentioned, such as recreational facilities) these benefits to individuals are not the reason for having the facilities in question. The justification for having them lies rather in the benefits that they bring to all. Military facilities and other public buildings have to be located somewhere, and may inevitably bring some benefits to people in that locale. The fact that some citizens get these benefits is not in itself a violation of equal concern. But if public facilities were consistently located in a certain region, without any other justification, this would seem to reflect a policy of favoring the interests of citizens in this region over the comparable interests of others. This policy would thus be a violation of the requirement of equal concern that I am describing.

Why should comparative levels of benefit matter in his way? The relevance of equality would be understandable if the good involved were competitive, so that a higher level of provision of the good gives some people an advantage over others. Education is a competitive good in this sense, but public services such as street paving and lighting are not competitive in this way. Better health does give some a competitive advantage over others, and access to health care can be justified on this basis as a component of equality of opportunity.[10] But this does not seem to me to be the only objection to unequal provision of medical care. The question is why unequal provision should be objectionable in the case of goods that are not competitive.

Indeed, a requirement of equal *treatment* would seem to be open to a version of the leveling down objection. As Joseph Raz puts it, "Egalitarian principles often lead to waste."[11] If it is impossible to provide a good equally to everyone, perhaps because there is not enough of it to go around, then an equalitarian principle would, Raz says, require giving it to no one.

This objection derives its plausibility from the particular way in which Raz understands egalitarian principles. He takes the paradigmatic form of such principles to be: "All Fs who do not have G have a right to G if some Fs have G."[12] This formulation differs in several important ways from the requirement of equal concern as I understand it. First, egalitarian principles as Raz states them apply simply to what goods people *have*, however this may have come about. By contrast, the requirement of equal concern that I am defending applies only to the *provision* of goods

---

[10] As Norman Daniels has argued. See his *Just Health Care*.
[11] *The Morality of Freedom*, 227.   [12] Raz, *Morality of Freedom*, 225.

by a single agent. Second, as I have said, equal concern does not always require that an agent provide individuals with equal amounts of a good. Unequal provision of some benefit is a violation of equal concern only if this would be unjustified if the interests of all those affected were given appropriate weight. Inequality need not be incompatible with equal concern if there is not enough of a good to benefit everyone equally, or if it is otherwise impossible, or difficult, or even, as I have said, particularly expensive, to supply some with the same level of benefit as others. This flexibility in the requirement of equal concern seems to me to handle the cases that give Raz's charge of wastefulness its initial plausibility.

The way in which this is so can be brought out more clearly by considering a different objection. The fact that unequal treatment is compatible with the requirement of equal concern when this inequality is supported by "good reasons" may seem to suggest that the requirement of equal concern that I am defending is only a *pro tanto* requirement, which is overridden in cases of the kinds I have described. This may seem particularly troubling in the case of some goods, such as protection against wrongful conviction. In response, I need to say more about the kind of balancing of interests that is involved in applying the requirement of equal concern.

The kind of concern that is morally required in cases of the kind I am discussing has two aspects, one non-comparative, the other comparative. A policy can involve objectionable lack of concern for some people because it is justified in a way that does not give their interests *sufficient* weight in relation to other values, or because it gives their interests *less* weight than the similar interests of other people. These two kinds of objections are illustrated by the example of procedural safeguards against wrongful conviction. A legal system can be open to objection because it does not give defendants the level of protection that is required—that is to say, if it does not give their interests in being protected against wrongful conviction sufficient weight in relation to the costs of providing these safeguards. But, as I argued, a legal system can also be open to objection if, even though it provides sufficient protection for all, it provides a higher level of protection for some people, if this indicates that it places greater weight on the protection of their interests.

Considerations that provide "good reason" for treatment that would otherwise be ruled out can therefore do this in either of two ways. These considerations can be good enough reason to provide some people with less than the minimum level of a good because they outweigh the reasons for providing the good at that level. What it takes to be a good reason for doing this will, obviously, vary with the importance of the good in question. It is one thing to outweigh the interest people have in an adequate level of street repaving, but it would be much more difficult to outweigh the interest people have in not being wrongly convicted of a crime. The point is just that when there are such reasons the failure to provide the good at the minimum level normally required does not reflect a failure to give sufficient weight to individuals' interest in having this good.

A second question is how some considerations can be good reason for providing more of a good to some than to others (where both are above the minimum level), and what is required in order for this to be the case. A policy that has the effect of providing unequal levels of a certain good might be supported by reasons that are unrelated to the benefit that this good brings to the affected individuals. For example, the roads in one area might need to be of higher quality in order to be used by trucks serving an industrial plant in that area. Or some residents might get better broadband access because of the wiring needed by a scientific research establishment that is nearby. Providing better services when these reasons apply would not violate the requirement of equal concern since the justification for doing this would not involve giving greater weight to the interests of some than to comparable interests of others.

The point is that when considerations justify unequal provision of some good in these ways they do not do this by outweighing the requirement of equal concern itself. Rather, the way that these considerations are balanced against the interests of individuals shows that these interests are receiving equal consideration even when the benefits provided are not the same.

Bringing the balancing of competing considerations within the scope of the requirement of equal concern itself may seem to go too far.[13] Suppose, for example, that a much-needed military appropriations bill contains a provision requiring that all the facilities that it will pay for should be located in a certain region of the country. This provision favors

---

[13] I thank Jed Lewinsohn for raising this possible objection.

interests of the residents of that area, without any justification. So the bill would seem to violate the requirement of equal concern. But the provision is insisted on by legislators from the area that would benefit, who will otherwise block passage of the bill. If passing the bill rather than not is, on balance, justified, taking into account the interests of all citizens, then it would seem, after all, to be in accord with the requirement of equal concern, on the basis of the reasoning I have proposed. This apparent paradox can be explained by distinguishing between whether the bill itself satisfies the requirement of equal concern, and whether *passing the bill* meets this requirement, given the circumstances. I take it that the answer to the first question is "no" and the answer to the second question is "yes."

This example also provides a good occasion to guard against a way in which the name I have given to this requirement may be misleading. The expression "equal *concern*" might suggest that what is required is a certain attitude (of concern) on the part of certain agents. But this is not correct. Whether an action or policy satisfies the requirement of equal concern is a matter of the reasons supporting it—whether it can be justified taking the interests of all affected parties into account in the right way. And this is so, in the case just considered, whether we are applying this requirement to a policy or to a decision to enact that policy in certain circumstances. The requirement concerns the reasons supporting such a decision, not the attitudes of the person making it.

The fact that determining whether a policy is compatible with the requirement of equal concern involves balancing competing considerations against the interests of individuals in having the good in question may seem to risk collapsing this requirement into a non-comparative requirement to give each person's interests, like his or her Nozickean rights, due weight. But this is not the case. The requirement of equal concern, as I am interpreting it, retains its comparative character because in some instances (for certain agents with respect to certain individuals) giving the interests of these individuals *appropriate* weight requires not only giving these interests sufficient weight but also giving these interests *the same* weight as the interests of (certain) other individuals.

This raises the question of when this requirement of equal concern applies. I have said that it applies to agents who have an obligation to provide benefits to certain people. But what agents have such an obligation, and towards whom? I do not have a general answer to this question.

Fortunately, I do not believe that such an answer is needed for my current limited purposes. My aim in this book is to identify various objections to inequality and the ideas of equality, if any, on which these objections are based. The aim of the present chapter is to examine one particular such objection, namely the objection to inequalities on the grounds that they arise from violations of a requirement of equal concern. It is therefore enough for present purposes to provide grounds for believing that such obligations exist, and that they do explain a distinct class of objections to inequality.

The examples I have given seem to me to make it very plausible that governments, local and national, can have such obligations to their citizens, and that requirements of equal concern flow from these obligations. To give another example, if the schools in the western part of Germany today were better funded than those in the eastern part, this would give rise to an at least prima facie objection of unequal concern. But this objection would not have been plausible when East and West Germany were separate countries.

This argument by appeal to examples can be given some support by a sketch of why governments should be under such a requirement. If the powers that governments exercise, to make and enforce laws, and to require citizens to pay taxes, rest on the benefits that they provide for their citizens, these must be benefits for *all* of their citizens (all who are required to obey the law and to pay taxes). Otherwise the others would have no reason to accept this justification for these powers. And why should some citizens accept that the interests of others count for more than their interests in justifying government policies, which they are being asked to cooperate in supporting through taxes and compliance with other laws?

If I have made it plausible that governments are under such a requirement of equal concern toward their citizens, this would be enough to establish my main point in this chapter. I suspect, however, that obligations of this kind are not limited to governments Parents have such obligations of equal concern toward their children. But it does not seem to me that such a requirement of equal concern applies to individuals generally, even if they have obligations to aid those who are less fortunate than themselves. If I give a substantial sum to aid poor people in a certain country, I might be subject to a prioritarian objection that I should instead have contributed to help people elsewhere, because they are in greater need. But I am not, it seems to me, open to a charge of unequal concern because I provided aid to some people but not also to others who are equally in need.

It is an interesting question whether private institutions can have obligations of this kind, and when this might be the case. If a charity is set up to aid certain universities, for example, it is not open to objection for not giving equal weight to the needs of other universities. If a foundation is set up to provide research and treatment for a certain disease, it is not open to objection for not being concerned with those who suffer from other diseases. But it might be open to objection if, having solicited contributions and sought tax-free status on this general ground, it confined itself to providing aid only for people who live in a certain area, neglecting those who suffer from the same disease elsewhere. This objection would, however, seem to differ from the requirement of equal concern that applies in the case of governments, since it seems to be grounded in the claims of the donors, rather than being something owed to the beneficiaries.[14] A better example might be a labor union, set up and supported by its members. It seems plausible to say both that the union is subject to a requirement that its decisions and policies should be justifiable taking the interests of all its members into account and counting them equally, and that this requirement of equal concern is owed to it members, who in this case are both beneficiaries and contributors.

Where such a requirement of equal concern for the interests of those to whom such an obligation is owed exists, this requirement of impartiality comes with a permission of *partiality*, to be concerned more with the interests of these individuals than with comparable interests of others, toward whom this obligation is not owed. This raises the question of whether this partiality is compatible with what I called in Chapter 1 basic moral equality—the idea that everyone matters morally. I believe that these ideas are in fact compatible. There is no general moral requirement on us as individuals to give equal weight to the interests of everyone who counts morally in every decision we make. This would be impossibly constraining and probably even impossible.

---

[14] I am grateful to Andrew Gold for pointing this out.

It might be more plausible to claim that national governments have such an obligation of concern for the interests of individuals beyond their borders. More strongly, it might be claimed that we as individuals have such an obligation, and that one justification for governments is that they provide us with a way of fulfilling this obligation in a way that is more efficient than individual action and not intrusive in the way that I have said that a general obligation on individuals would be.

Even if there were such an obligation of equal concern with regard to certain goods, such as, perhaps, the conditions required for good health and the economic goods required for a decent life, governments would still have other special obligations of equal concern toward their citizens with respect to other goods. These would include goods that need to be provided locally and subject to local decision, such as street paving and education, and, generally, to further goods that governments are assigned responsibility for through democratic procedures.

Whether national governments have a broader obligation to provide some goods to those beyond their borders, giving rise to a requirement of equal concern for those toward whom this particular obligation is owed, would depend on whether such an obligation is justified by the fact that the consequences of its absence are morally unsupportable. The claim that this is so would depend in part on the claim that such an obligation is an effective way of preventing these consequences. This will depend in turn on which goods can effectively be provided by outsiders.

This brings me back to the contrast that I drew at the outset between international disparities in life expectancy and inequalities of life expectancy within a single country. It might be argued that international differences in life expectancy raise questions of unequal treatment in a different way. Even if these differences do not arise from the failure of any existing single institution to give equal weight to the needs of various people for medical care and other conditions of good health, it might be said that there needs to be some institution with an obligation to all to provide these goods.

This would be a two-step argument to a conclusion about objectionable inequality. The first step is the (non-comparative) claim that such an institution with a universal obligation is necessary in order for the interests of many people to be given sufficient weight (and that it would be an effective way of ensuring that these interests are served). The second step would be that international disparities of the kind that now exist would constitute a violation of the requirement of equal treatment such an institution would have. But even if this is correct, it would remain the case, I believe, that under present circumstances what is objectionable about international disparities in life expectancy is not the inequality involved.

3

Status Inequality

Caste systems and societies marked by racial or sexual discrimination are obvious examples of objectionable inequality. Societies of this kind may be open to objection on a number of grounds. In this chapter I will be concerned with one such objection, based on the inequality of status that they involve. My aim is to examine this objection in more detail, and to consider how, and under what conditions, economic inequalities can be objectionable on similar grounds. I will also consider whether a thoroughly meritocratic society might be open to objections of this kind.

In societies with caste and class distinctions, and in societies marked by racial discrimination, some people are denied access to valued forms of employment simply on grounds of their birth. They are often also denied basic political rights, such as the right to vote and to participate in politics, and, as I said in Chapter 2, often not provided with important public services that are owed to all. In addition, they are viewed as ineligible for what I will call *associational goods* in relation to people outside of their group. For example, they are seen by people in other groups as less eligible to be co-workers, potential friends, possible marriage partners, or even neighbors.

People who are discriminated against in these ways are denied important opportunities for no good reason. This could be wrong even if it were due to mere arbitrariness or, in the case of public services, due to favoritism for political allies of government officials. But those who are subject to discrimination in the sense I am concerned with are denied these goods on the basis of the widely held view that certain facts about them, such as their race, gender, or religion, make them less entitled to these goods than others are. The fact that people are subject to a widely held view of inferiority of this kind—of being less entitled to important goods and opportunities, and less suitable for valued forms of personal relationship—is a distinctive feature of discrimination as I am understanding it.

The wrongfulness of discrimination depends on the fact that the characteristics on which it is based, such as race and gender, do not justify the attitudes and differences in treatment that it involves. Perhaps sensing this, those who discriminate often appeal to empirical generalizations that may seem to offer better justification, such as that members of the group discriminated against are untrustworthy, or lazy, or that they do not have the abilities that are required for the roles from which they are excluded. These generalizations are generally false. But even if they were true they would not justify the forms of treatment that discrimination involves. Withholding trust, or positions of responsibility, from a person on the grounds that he is untrustworthy requires evidence that he in particular is untrustworthy, and denying a position to someone on the grounds that she lacks the relevant abilities requires evidence of her actual lack of ability. Statistical facts about the group to which a person belongs do not always have the relevant justificatory force.[1]

Discrimination of this kind is made worse if the members of the group that is discriminated against come to see this treatment and the attitudes that it expresses as justified. This would be a blow to their "self-respect," or "self-esteem" in the sense Rawls speaks of: "a person's sense of his own value, his secure conviction that his conception of the good, his plan of life, is worth carrying out" and "a confidence in one's ability, so far as it is within one's power, to fulfill one's intentions."[2]

But a feeling of inferiority, or loss of self-esteem, is not essential to the objection I am considering. This objection applies whenever enough people in a society hold these views of superiority and inferiority, with the result that the practices of exclusion and preference I have described exist and are stable. It is of course possible for the individuals who are discriminated against to come to affirm the roles and associated values of their status, and mistakenly find self-respect (in Rawls's sense) in fulfilling these roles. They would then not have the experience of humiliation I just described, but the discrimination involved would still be objectionable on the grounds I am presently concerned with.

---

[1] It is a difficult question when and why statistical evidence is insufficient justification for certain forms of treatment. For discussion, see Judith Thomson, "Liability and Individualized Evidence," and David Enoch, Levi Specter, and Talia Fisher, "Statistical Evidence, Sensitivity, and the Legal Value of Knowledge." I am grateful to Frances Kamm and to Paul Weithman for pressing on me on this point.

[2] *A Theory of Justice*, 2nd edn, 386.

Whether members of a group that is discriminated against experience this as a blow to their self-respect or self-esteem, or instead find self-respect and self-esteem in the fulfillment of the roles assigned to them, many members of the groups that are not discriminated against in this way are likely to regard the fact that they do *not* have the characteristics of this group as a particularly important fact about them, and as a bulwark of their self-respect—a reason for thinking their lives are worthwhile and their projects worth pursuing. As Rousseau pointed out, there is likely to be a pathology of attitudes on both sides, the pathology of valuing or disvaluing one's life and activities for inappropriate reasons, and governing one's attitudes and behavior toward others by these mistaken reasons.[3]

Eliminating discrimination or other forms of status inequality would not be objectionable "leveling down"—making some people worse off without benefitting anyone else. It would deprive some people of a feeling of superiority that they may value. But this is not something that they could complain of losing. So it would not make anyone worse off in a morally relevant sense, and it would benefit those who had been discriminated against.[4] Being denied the goods I have mentioned for no good reason, and being subject to attitudes of inferiority of the kinds I have described are things people have good reason to object to. Their objections are not mere envy of what others have.

Social practices of the kind I have been describing are thus subject to three kinds of objection. First, many individuals are barred from important goods and opportunities for no good reason. Second, both those who discriminate and those who are discriminated against are deprived of the important good of being able to relate to each other as equals. Third, many of the individuals in such a society are led to value (or disvalue) their own lives and activities for reasons that are not good reasons. Those in the "superior" groups may base their sense of worth, falsely, on this superior status. Those who are held to be inferior, if they accept this judgment, inappropriately disvalue themselves and their activities. If those who are discriminated against embrace and base their sense of worth on fulfilling the roles they are assigned as "the only ones appropriate

---

[3] *Discourse on the Origins of Inequality.*

[4] To say that such losses are morally irrelevant is not to deny that they are psychologically powerful, and can be exploited politically to bad effect.

for them," given what they are, they base this positive valuation on false reasons.

These objections vary in the degree to which they are egalitarian. The second objection is the most clearly egalitarian, based as it is on the value of individuals' relating to one another as equals. The first objection is a matter of justice—the unjust denial of important forms of opportunity. But this objection may or may not be egalitarian. As I pointed out in Chapter 2, failure to provide these goods can be a non-comparative wrong, a violation of individuals' rights, as well as a comparative wrong, showing unequal concern. The problem identified by the third objection, that individuals value themselves and others in mistaken ways, is, at the most basic level, an error about "the good," rather than "the right." Insofar as the injustice with which the first objection is concerned occurs only because individuals make this evaluative error, this is a kind of dependence of "the right" on (prevalent ideas about) "the good." As G. A. Cohen would put it, it is a case in which the achievement of justice depends on the ethos of a society.[5]

I turn now to the question of how economic inequality can lead to objectionable inequality in status, as Adam Smith observed when he said that it is an objection to economic conditions if they make it the case that some individuals cannot go out in public without shame.[6] We need to look more closely at how economic inequality can produce objectionable effects of this kind.

The mechanism through which this happens, I take it, is this. The ways that individuals dress, how they live, what they own or can consume—what kind of car they drive, for example, or whether they even have a car, or whether they have a computer—may mark them as eligible or ineligible for certain roles and, particularly, as more or less eligible for associational goods of the kind I have mentioned. Since their access to these things depends on the amounts of money they have, economic inequality can have effects of this kind on the status of those who have less.

---

[5] G. A. Cohen, "Where the Action is," 10–15, et passim. The forms of ethos that Cohen was particularly concerned with were attitudes about the right—about what individuals were or were not entitled to do. I am emphasizing instead prevailing ideas about what is worth valuing, and in what way, and suggesting that these are important in a way that is similar to what Cohen suggested.

[6] An Inquiry into the Nature and Causes of the Wealth of Nations, 351–2.

These effects are clearly described by Jiwei Ci.[7] Ci distinguishes what he calls three "stakes of poverty," by which he means, I think, three ways in which being poor can be a bad thing for a person. Subsistence poverty occurs when lack of money threatens a person's ability to meet the needs of physical survival. Status poverty occurs when lack of money makes it impossible for a person to live in the way that is required, in his or her society, in order to be respected. Agency poverty occurs when a person's lack of money makes it impossible for him or her to function in the way that is required, in his or her society, to be a "normal functioning agent"—to have a job, say, or to do other things that are essential in that society to obtain the things that a person has reason to want. In our societies, avoiding agency poverty may involve such things as having a credit card, an address, a telephone, and perhaps access to the internet. All three aspects of poverty threaten poor individuals' self-respect in something like the terms in which Rawls defines it: a secure sense of the worth of one's life plan and the ability to carry out such a plan.

As Ci points out, these three reasons why being poor can be a bad thing for a person are related but separable. An ascetic, who endures subsistence poverty by choice, may suffer no loss of agency, or of status. Ascetics may be admired, and seen as more than usually competent individuals. In Mao's China, Ci says, subsistence poverty did not convey lack of status, but rather marked a person as a particularly committed participant in the Communist struggle for a better China, and being wealthier could bring suspicion and stigma. In today's China, by contrast, having a car is an important status symbol, and living like a peasant marks a person for disrespect.[8] Similarly, one can experience status poverty while still having the full feeling of functioning as an agent: having a job, participating in the economy as a consumer, being a parent, and so on.

To illustrate this point in an American context, in a recent online editorial an African American woman responded to criticism of poor people who, it was said, "waste money" on luxury goods such as iPhones.[9] The woman described how appearing in recognizable "designer" clothes with a "designer" handbag, enabled her mother to get welfare payments

---

[7] Jiwei Ci, "Agency and Other Stakes of Poverty."
[8] "Agency and Other Stakes of Poverty," 128–30.
[9] M. T. Cottom, "Why do Poor People 'Waste' Money on Luxury Goods?"

restored for the grand-daughter of her neighbor after her neighbor had simply been turned away at the office. This is not, she writes, a matter of being merely presentable (i.e. clean and not smelling, in clothes that are not ragged) but rather looking like *someone*—like a person who needs to be treated with respect. The writer's point, I believe, is just that, for a person who is poor, especially a black person, having certain luxury goods can be crucial to avoid what Ci calls status poverty *and* agency poverty—crucial to being able to function well in society.

What Ci calls status poverty and agency poverty are bad for a person for different reasons. Agency poverty has to do with the fact that a lack of money can prevent a person from doing things that are essential to life in a given society. These effects depend on how the society in question is organized, and what makes them bad are the reasons individuals in such a society have to want to be able to do the things in question. The way in which poverty can make this impossible need not depend on any discriminatory attitudes of other people in the society. Status poverty, on the other hand, depends on such attitudes. Being seen by others as inferior and undesirable as a candidate for various relationships is a bad thing in itself. As the example I just gave illustrates, however, being seen as inferior in this way can also interfere with being able to do things one needs to do in order to function effectively in a society. Poverty can interfere with agency *by* marking a person as of low status. But poverty can interfere with agency in other ways, and low status can be objectionable for other reasons.

These ideas capture what I think Adam Smith must have had in mind in the passage I quoted. The feeling that Smith says is occasioned by poverty involves believing that others see one (and perhaps even seeing oneself) as ineligible, or less eligible than others, for valued roles and various associational goods. It can also involve being unable to function effectively as a "normal agent" in one's society, leading even to the sense that one is a failure in life.

I said earlier in discussing discrimination and caste systems that the harms that these systems cause are good reasons for eliminating the positions of privilege. If economic inequalities cause similar harms, then this would be a *pro tanto* reason for preferring a situation without those inequalities, even if this would reduce the economic well-being of some or all. As Ci points out, however, the harms of status poverty result from economic inequality only given certain prevailing attitudes. So these harms also provide direct reasons for changing those attitudes, if that is possible. Even if the distribution of economic advantages were left unchanged, if feeling superior to others is one of the reasons people desire wealth and income, at least beyond a certain point, then this change in attitudes would take something away from the better off. But this would not be a loss they have any claim to object to.

This is a mirror image of the familiar charge of envy. The charge of envy is an objection to demands for reducing inequality, claiming that these demands merely express unjustifiable desires that others not have more than you do. What I have just described, by contrast, is an objection to *resistance* to reducing inequality, claiming that this resistance merely expresses unjustifiable desires to have more than others do.

Here again we see the interrelation of the right and ideas of the good. The social attitudes that mediate between economic inequality and status harms consist, as I said earlier, in widespread evaluative error. People regard differences in income and forms of consumption as having a kind of importance that those differences do not in fact have. One way of avoiding status harms that I just mentioned would consist in correcting these errors, if this were possible.

I doubt that it is always possible. But imagine for a moment a society in which at least some of these errors are corrected. Near the end of his paper on affirmative action, Thomas Nagel writes, "When racial and sexual injustice have been reduced, we shall still be left with the great injustice of the smart and the dumb, who are so differently rewarded for comparable effort."[10] Nagel mentions differences in economic reward, but the same thing might be said about differences in esteem, and it is these I want to focus on.

So imagine a society in which there is no discrimination on grounds of race, sex, or other accidents of birth aside from talents. There are, I will assume, some offices and positions that everyone in the society regards as desirable to hold. This is not only because of the economic rewards attached to them (and we might even assume that these rewards are very modest or even non-existent). Rather, these positions are seen as desirable because of the opportunities they offer to exercise developed talents in a valuable way, and perhaps also because these positions

[10] "The Policy of Preference," 104.

constitute recognition that those who qualify for them are, along various important dimensions, more successful than others in developing and exercising abilities that everyone has reason to value and to wish to have. I assume that people are selected for these positions purely on the basis of merit, with no discrimination or favoritism, and that everyone recognizes this to be the case. One might even say that it is true, and believed to be true, that the people who occupy these positions *deserve* them. This will be so at least in the institutional sense of 'desert': they are assigned these positions and rewards by institutions that are justified. But insofar as these positions constitute appropriate recognition for certain forms of excellence, they might be said to be deserved in a deeper, non-institutional sense: those who occupy these positions have characteristics that, in themselves, make this form of recognition appropriate.[11]

My question is whether the differences recognized in such a society would involve status harms of the kind I have been discussing. If so, then it would seem that a thoroughly meritocratic society would have some of the faults of a caste society.[12] There would, of course, be some mobility that is lacking in a caste society—a possibility for talented children of any class to "move up" to more desirable positions. Everyone in the society will, I have assumed, believe that it is a good thing to have the talents that qualify one for one of these positions, and a misfortune to lack them. All parents, for example, will have reason to want their children to have these talents. But why don't these attitudes amount to a kind of objectionable status hierarchy?

These attitudes do not, I am assuming, involve any kind of factual error. Even if they do not involve error, however, or *especially* if they do not, won't those who lack these talents feel a justified lack of status? How could this be avoided? This poses a problem: Can we recognize that certain talents are very much worth developing, that we all have reason to try to develop them in ourselves and our children, and that social roles and positions that allow people to exercise these talents for the benefit of all of us are quite justified, without at the same time endorsing a society in which some will feel a justified, and objectionable, lack of status and self-esteem? Rousseau responded to this dilemma by rejecting the first

---

[11] I assess these different ideas of desert in Chapter 8.

[12] A question raised by the British sociologist Michael Young, in his dystopian fable, *The Rise of the Meritocracy*.

premise: he held that people valued special accomplishments only as a way of feeling superior to others. So there would be nothing lost in giving these up, if we could do so. (He thought we could not.)

Unlike Rousseau, however, I believe that evaluative attitudes of this kind can be justified. Some forms of accomplishment are worth striving for. It is appropriate to feel pleased if we attain them, and to feel regret if we do not. So I must face the question of how objectionable effects of the kind I have described might be avoided, or whether they must simply be accepted as a fact of life.

I said earlier that all parents in the society I was imagining wanted their children to develop the abilities that would qualify them for special positions, by getting into the best universities, for example, and that people would all be disappointed not to have these abilities. It matters a great deal here, however, not just *that* certain abilities and accomplishments are valued in a society but *in what way* they are valued—what kind of significance this value has in people's lives and their relations with each other.[13] I have assumed that people in the society I am imagining value the kind of abilities that qualify one to do well in higher education. They want their children to develop such abilities, and are disappointed if they do not. Indeed, as we will see in discussing equality of opportunity, it is important, if children are to have the kind of opportunity that they have reason to want, that they grow up in an environment in which they see the development of these abilities as something they have reason to strive for.

But it is one thing to see certain abilities as desirable, and quite a different thing—an evaluative error—to be crushed if one does not have them oneself, or if one's children do not qualify for the best universities. Even if people have reason to want their children to have talents that will qualify them for desirable positions, they also have good reason to believe that there are other things worth doing—other lives that are worth living and that one should be content to live. Failure to appreciate this is

---

[13] On the importance of distinguishing different ways of being valuable, see chapter 2 of my *What We Owe to Each Other*, esp. 99–103. My argument here and elsewhere relies on the view that there is such a thing as valuing certain accomplishments excessively, or in the wrong way, and that it can be an error to fail to see certain options as worth pursuing. But I am not relying on the stronger thesis that there is always a fact of the matter about how valuable certain options are and about which one a given person has most reason to pursue. I thank Joseph Fishkin for calling this point to my attention.

another kind of evaluative error. An environment in which one is led to see a plurality of lives as having value is another part of the kind of opportunity that everyone should, ideally, have.[14] When we think of a perfectly meritocratic society as unavoidably involving an objectionable hierarchy this may be because we are imagining a society in which most people make this error, and are excessively concerned with particular forms of merit.

We may also think of such a society as one in which those who have this kind of merit feel superior to those who do not, and the latter feel inferior and "looked down upon." This is a further kind of evaluative error. Valuing certain abilities and accomplishments, and being pleased that one has them, need not involve believing that this makes one superior to others, or more important than they are. But while this distinction may be clear in theory, it is difficult to separate these attitudes in practice, and the difficulty of doing so is a serious problem. On the one hand, one wants children in all parts of society to see the value of doing well in school and qualifying for higher education. On the other hand, they should not feel inferior to those who do well in these ways, or believe that such people look down on them (whatever the actual attitudes of these people may be). Superiority and inferiority of this kind is suggested by Nagel's words "the smart and the dumb," whether or not this was his intent. Such attitudes of superiority and inferiority are widespread in our society, for understandable reasons, and the resulting feelings of inferiority can be exploited with poisonous political consequences.

Separating a recognition of the value of abilities and accomplishments from feelings of superiority and inferiority is made more difficult by the role that these abilities play in people's everyday activities and in their relations with each other. It is not unreasonable to prefer associating with people who value the things one values and who have the knowledge and skills that are required to engage in their pursuit. Rawls's idea of non-comparing groups may be seen as a way of recognizing this difficulty and attempting to mitigate its effects.

Rawls says that even if a society rewards certain abilities by having positions of advantage, licensed by the Difference Principle, for which individuals are chosen under conditions of fair equality of opportunity,

---

[14] This point is emphasized by Joseph Fishkin. See *Bottlenecks*, chapter 3.

these differences in reward need not lead to loss of self-respect. This is so, he says, partly because people will tend to form "non-comparing groups" in which they associate mainly with others who have similar interests and abilities. In order to protect people against a loss of self-respect (a loss of confidence in the worth of their plans of life and in their ability to carry them out) what is required, Rawls says, "is that there should be for each person at least one community of shared interests to which he belongs and where he finds his endeavors confirmed by his associates."[15] He also writes, "the plurality of associations in a well-ordered society, each with its secure internal life, tends to reduce the visibility, or at least the painful visibility, of variations in men's prospects. For we tend to compare our circumstances with those of others in our group, or in positions we regard as relevant to our aspirations."[16]

This might seem evasive—a way of concealing the problem rather than a solution. It would be an evasion if the differences that were being concealed were differences that are in themselves unjust. But Rawls's point is rather that even inequalities that are just may provoke regret and unhappy comparisons if one's nose is constantly rubbed into them in one's daily life. This will not happen, Rawls says, if such non-comparing groups arise. It may also make a difference which kinds of inequalities are in question. Rawls may be talking in part about differences in income and wealth, but his main concern, and my concern here, is with individuals' sense of failure at turning out to be less good than they have reason to want to be at things that are worth striving for. The shielding effect of non-comparing groups seems less controversial as a way of dealing with the latter problem than with unhappiness due to economic differences.

However one may judge this, non-comparing groups are a very real phenomenon, and I will close this chapter by speculating that they are relevant in two ways to the recent explosion of economic inequality in our societies. Whatever reasons there may be for objecting to this growth in inequality, the idea that the extreme wealth and incomes of "the one percent" give rise to feelings of injured status and loss of self-respect among members of the 99 percent seems to me not among them. Judging first from my own experience, I certainly do not feel any distress at the fact that I cannot live in the style to which they seem to have become

---

[15] *A Theory of Justice*, 2nd edn, 388.   [16] *A Theory of Justice*, 2nd edn, 470.

accustomed. Perhaps this is just because life provides me with many other supports for my self-respect. So perhaps things are different for those who have much less than I do. But I doubt this. I would speculate that the economic inequality in our societies that causes status harms is mainly the inequality between people like me—successful educated professionals—and those who have less, especially, as I have noted above, those who are truly poor, and lack education. These effects may be reduced by the fact that we belong to non-comparing groups, but I doubt that they are totally erased.

It does seem plausible, however, that my own lack of distress about the difference between my life and that of the super rich is due in part to the fact that we belong to different non-comparing groups. The way they live does not make me subject to status poverty or agency poverty, because their life does not set any norms of expectation for me. But it does set a norm *for them*, and this can have important effects. I have no desire to have that much money, or the things it can buy, such as private jets. But the very rich do desire these things, apparently, and I imagine that this is in no small part because others to whom they compare themselves have and desire these things. Externally non-comparing groups are loci of internal comparison.

This may be relevant at least to that part of the recent growth of inequality in the United States that consists of a great increase in the compensation of corporate executives. Criticism of the levels of executive compensation in the United States has led to two changes in the practice through which the compensation of corporate executives is determined.[17] The first is that facts about executives' compensation have become much more publicly available. A second is that compensation committees increasingly hire outside consultants to advise them in deciding on the compensation for their executives each year. One thing these consultants do is to provide "comparables"—that is to say, reports of the compensation given to executives in companies the corporation in question would like to compare itself to.

It might have been hoped that these two changes—greater transparency and the use of outside consultants, to avoid the appearance of board members simply favoring their friends—would to some degree slow the growth of executive compensation. But the reverse seems to have

---

[17] In what follows I draw on Josh Bivens and Lawrence Mishel, "The Pay of Corporate Executives and Financial Professionals as Evidence of Rents in Top 1 Percent Incomes."

occurred, and it seems reasonable to speculate that this is because these measures actually have escalating effects on compensation. One effect is that firms compare themselves to other firms that are doing as well or better than they are, and feel that what they offer their executives must at least "keep up" with what these other firms are offering. Another effect that seems to me likely is that these measures solidify the sense, on the part of executives, that they *deserve* these levels of reward, since they take the publicly available facts about what other executives are receiving as a benchmark, indicating what people *should* get for (successfully) doing the kind of work that they do.[18]

I will argue in Chapter 8 that ideas about what level of economic reward people deserve for performing certain jobs are largely matters of social convention, and are without any moral basis. Insofar as these social conventions exist, however, it is not surprising that people feel they deserve what they see others like them regularly receiving.[19] This may help to explain the behavior of both those who demand and expect these high levels of compensation and those who grant them bonuses and pay increases. But when we recognize the conventional nature of these ideas of desert, it is clear that they have no moral weight, however firmly they may be held.

This may seem inconsistent with what I said earlier, when I took status poverty and agency poverty quite seriously, as morally weighty objections to poverty, even while acknowledging that they depend on the prevailing attitudes of the society in question. But there is no inconsistency here. In neither case does a social convention make it the case that a person deserves what the convention holds to be appropriate. This is what I just denied in the case of the expectations of the well to do. In both cases failure to meet the conventionally established standards involves a cost. But the status poverty and agency poverty endured by the poor involve costs that are much more serious than what the very rich suffer by not being able to live in the style that those around them may have come to expect.

---

[18] Gregory Mankiw, for example, defends high levels of compensation on grounds of desert in "Defending the One Percent."

[19] Thomas Piketty suggests that changes in social norms about acceptable rates of compensation for senior managers have been an important factor behind the recent rise in inequality, especially in the United States and the United Kingdom. See *Capital in the Twenty-First Century*, 264–5.

To summarize. In this chapter I have tried to describe what seems to us objectionable about societies marked by discrimination. The evils of such a society involve, I argued, the unjustified denial of important goods, including what I have called associational goods.

I went on to explain how economic inequality can produce status harms like those that are part of societies marked by discrimination. These harms depend not only on economic inequality but also on prevailing attitudes about the significance of certain goods, attitudes that involve evaluative errors. I then considered whether similar harms might persist, without such errors, in a society in which there was no discrimination and in fact full of equality of opportunity. I considered Rawls's idea of non-comparing groups as a way of avoiding such harms.

The tendency behind the idea of non-comparing groups—the tendency of people to associate mainly with others of similar status within whatever hierarchies exist in their society—is a sociological phenomenon that can occur in just and unjust societies alike. Rawls's concern was with a just society. He appealed to the tendency to form non-comparing groups as a factor that would minimize harms to self-respect in a society that met his criteria of justice as far as economic distribution was concerned, and in which the relevant hierarchies would therefore mainly involve degrees of success measured in terms of non-economic values. I have suggested that in unjust societies, with high levels of economic inequality, the tendency to form non-comparing groups can foster the development of unjustified ideas of desert and entitlement.

Moreover, this is not the only way in which this tendency can have negative effects in unequal societies. If those who are well-off associate mainly with others of the same economic level, they will have less understanding of the lives and needs of those who have less, and are likely to be less sympathetic to their plight.[20] This can make them more likely to form moralistic views of the kind I will discuss in Chapter 5, less willing to support policies that are needed to provide substantive opportunity for all members of society, and in general less willing to meet the requirements of equal concern that I discussed in Chapter 2. This means that they will be less likely to perform properly in their roles as public officials and as citizens and voters, in ways I will discuss in Chapter 6.

---

[20] Avoiding these tendencies is a main feature of what Danielle Allen calls a "connected society." See her "Toward a Connected Society."

4

Procedural Fairness

Equality of opportunity, understood as the idea that individuals' chances of economic success should not depend on their family's economic status, is widely agreed to be morally important. But surprisingly little is said about why this is so. In this chapter and the next I will investigate this question. My aim will be to identify the complex mixture of moral ideas involved in the idea of equality of opportunity and to examine the relations between them, thus providing a moral anatomy of this topic. I will be particularly concerned with the degree to which the various considerations supporting equality of opportunity are themselves egalitarian, and with the ideas of equality that they involve.

Because equality of opportunity is compatible with unequal rewards, and even presupposes them, and because it appears to say nothing about how these unequal rewards should be limited or justified, it has something of a bad name among many egalitarians. It may be said that equality of opportunity is not really an egalitarian doctrine at all, or that it is a myth, promulgated in order to make unacceptable inequalities seem acceptable. The idea of equality of opportunity is often misused in this way, and this misuse is something we need to be on guard against. Properly understood, however, equality of opportunity is not a justification for inequality but an independent requirement that must be satisfied in order for inequalities that are justified in some other way to be just. If this requirement is taken seriously, it can have strong egalitarian implications. So the bad reputation I mentioned may be undeserved, at least in part. In order to assess this debate, we need to identify the arguments for the requirement of equality of opportunity and make clear how this requirement should be understood.

I will view equality of opportunity as part of a three-level response to an objection to inequality. Suppose that a person objects to the fact that he or she is not as well off as others are, economically or in some other way. A satisfactory response to this complaint, I believe, needs to involve three claims.

1. *Institutional Justification*: It is justified to have an institution that generates inequalities of this kind.
2. *Procedural Fairness:* The process through which it came about that others received this advantage while the person who is complaining did not was procedurally fair.
3. *Substantive Opportunity:* There is no wrong involved in the fact that the complainant did not have the necessary qualifications or other means to do better in this process.

These claims constitute what I will refer to as a *three-level justification* for inequality. The key to the idea of equality of opportunity, I believe, lies in understanding the nature and basis of these claims, and the relations between them.

A claim of institutional justification can take a number of different forms. It might be claimed, for example, that inequalities are justified simply by the fact that they arise from interactions between individuals exercising their property and contract rights. Alternatively, inequality-generating institutions might be held to be justified on the grounds that they give individuals what they deserve. I mention these forms of institutional justification for purposes of completeness and contrast, although I do not endorse either of them, for reasons that I will discuss in Chapters 7 and 8. The institutional justifications I will be most concerned with claim that inequality-generating institutions are justified by the effects of having institutions of this kind.

One familiar justification of this kind claims that institutions that generate high levels of pay for individuals in certain positions, such as corporate executives, are justified because these rewards attract talented individuals, and thus contribute to the productivity of these institutions. Rawls's Difference Principle is another justification of this general form. It holds that features of an institution that generate inequalities are just only if they benefit those who are worse off, and could not be eliminated without making some people still worse off. This justification differs from the justification appealing simply to increased productivity because it has an explicit distributional element: that inequalities are justified only if they make those who have less better off than the worst off would be under any more equal distribution of benefits. What these two forms of justification have in common is that according to both the justifiability of positions to which special advantages are attached depends on benefits that flow if those positions are filled by individuals with abilities of the right kind.

The claims of procedural fairness that I will be concerned with follow from particular institutional justifications, and the relevant standards of procedural fairness depend on the nature of this justification. If inequalities were justified when they arose from the exercise of individuals' property rights, then the only procedural requirement would be that particular inequalities actually arose in this way—that no fraud or theft was involved, for example. And if an institution is justified by the fact that it gives individuals what they deserve, then particular unequal benefits are justified only if the institution that produced them was actually responding to desert of the appropriate kind. Finally, in the class of cases I will be interested in, if the justification for the institutional mechanisms that generated inequalities lies in the beneficial consequences of having inequalities of this kind, procedural fairness requires that these unequal positions be assigned in a way that actually leads to these benefits.

So, if positions of special advantage are justified by the beneficial consequences that will result if they are filled by individuals with certain abilities, then procedural fairness requires that individuals be chosen for these positions on the grounds that they have these abilities. If the positions are not filled in this way, then the positions are not functioning in a way that fits with the justification for them. I will call this the institutional account of procedural fairness.

This account applies most directly when positions of advantage are filled through a process that involves decisions by individuals or institutional committees, such as decisions about which individuals to hire or to admit to educational institutions. Procedural fairness requires that these decisions be made on grounds that are "rationally related" to the justification for these positions—that is to say, to the ways in which these positions promote the purposes of the institutions of which they are a part.

Given the importance of employment as a source of economic benefits, and the importance of forms of education as gateways to many desirable forms of employment, this covers an important range of cases, which it is natural to focus on. But it is important to recognize that these are not the only inequality-generating mechanisms about which questions of equality of opportunity arise. Some people may become richer than others by starting limited liability corporations, for example, or by acquiring patents or other forms of intellectual property. If these inequality-generating mechanisms are justified by the economic benefits of a system that includes them, then complaints of procedural unfairness are in order if some people are excluded from taking advantage of these legal forms on grounds that are irrelevant to their economic function. (As we will see in Chapter 5, complaints can also be in order if some people lack the means to take advantage of these opportunities.)

Procedural fairness as I am describing it is based on the justification for certain inequalities. It may thus seem not to be an egalitarian notion, although the three-level justification that includes it is egalitarian in presupposing that the inequalities in question require justification. But the idea of procedural fairness has, historically, been the basis for objections to important forms of inequality.

Many cases of wrongful discrimination, for example, are wrong in part because they involve procedural unfairness of the kind I have just described. But this is not the only objection to familiar forms of discrimination, and not all forms of wrongful discrimination are wrong for this reason. Where a practice of racial discrimination exists, members of the disfavored group are systematically excluded from valued positions, and perhaps denied other associational goods, because they are viewed as inferior in ways that make them unsuitable for these goods or positions. As I argued in Chapter 3, such a practice is objectionable not only because it violates procedural fairness, but also because it is wrong for people to be stigmatized in this way. By contrast, nepotism, cronyism, and pure laziness in assessing applicants are procedurally unfair, even though they do not involve objectionable stigmatization.

The term 'discrimination' can be applied to a number of different things. If members of a certain political party are excluded from consideration for judgeships and other positions of advantage, it might be said that they are being "discriminated against." The objection to this would simply be one of procedural unfairness. Other cases commonly called discrimination might not involve either procedural unfairness or stigmatization. Failure to make public facilities accessible to people who are unable to walk, for example, would be discrimination against the handicapped in this broad sense. Even if it did not reflect a stigmatizing attitude toward disabled people, it would be objectionable simply as a violation of equal concern of the kind I discussed in Chapter 2: a failure to take into account, in the appropriate way, the interests of all.

What is common to all these cases is that they involve wrongful denial of some benefit or opportunity. The aim of my exercise in moral anatomy is to identify the various factors that can make such a denial wrongful. I have just mentioned three such factors: procedural unfairness, stigmatization, and failure of equal concern. All of these wrongs may be appropriately called discrimination in a broad sense. My purpose here has been to call attention to the fact that they are distinct wrongs that can occur independent of one another, and are wrong for different reasons.

When the inequalities to which equality of opportunity applies are justified by the benefits that will result if these positions are filled by individuals with the relevant talent, "equality of opportunity" does not require that everyone, talented or not, should be able to attain these positions. Rejecting the untalented is not unfair, or a form of discrimination. If the inequalities in question were not justified by such effects, or justified on grounds of desert, then there would be no basis for merit-based selection, because there would be no relevant idea of merit. If, for example, assigning someone the role of directing others solved some important coordination problem, but this administrative role required no special skill, then procedural fairness of the kind I am describing would not apply. If the role were seen as desirable, perhaps fairness might require assigning it by a lottery, to avoid objectionable favoritism. But this idea of fairness would be different from the one I am describing.

It should be emphasized, since it will be important in what follows, that the idea of merit or talent that is relevant to procedural fairness on an account of the kind I am discussing is an institution-dependent notion. That is to say, what counts as a talent (i.e. a valid basis for selection) depends on the justification of the institution in question and the nature and justification of the position within it for which individuals are being selected.

It is natural to think of talents as properties of an individual that have value independent of social institutions within which they are made use of or rewarded. It may be, for example, that musical ability of a certain kind is a valuable thing for an individual to have, and that it is therefore a good thing to have social institutions that allow for this ability to be developed and exercised. What counts as musical ability in a given society will of course vary, depending on the musical traditions of that society. But it at least makes sense to say that certain forms of musical ability are particularly valuable, and that it is therefore a good thing if the traditions of a society recognize this value and allow for the development of musical ability of this valuable kind.

But the talents that are relevant to procedural fairness need not, and generally will not, be like this.[1] The talents that are an appropriate basis of selection for a position of advantage are just those characteristics, whatever they may be, possession of which makes a person likely to perform in the position in question in a way that promotes the aims that provide the institutional justification for having that position.[2] In a few cases this justification may have to do with the independent value of certain abilities. A music school, for example, might be justified on the basis of the value of developing musical ability of a certain kind. But this is not the normal case. Skill at computer programming may or may not be valuable in itself. But what makes it a relevant basis of selection for a certain position is the fact, when it is a fact, that having individuals with that skill in that position will promote some other goal, such as having a website that enables citizens to get medical insurance.

What counts as a talent in the relevant sense will depend not only on the goals of the institution but also on the way in which this institution and the particular position in question are organized. If a position requires lifting heavy objects, then physical strength is an important form of ability. But if the job is done with a fork-lift truck then it is not. If succeeding in a particular job, or in a university course of study, requires one to understand French, then knowledge of French is a relevant ability. If everything is done in English, then it is not. This dependence on the goals that justify an institution and on the way it is organized to promote these goals are what I mean by saying that the idea of talent, or ability, that is relevant to procedural fairness is "institution-dependent."

---

[1] They would be like this if the institutions giving rise to inequalities were justified on the grounds that they give people what they deserve, in a sense that is independent of these institutions. I thank Ben Bagley for calling this possibility to my attention. I will argue in Chapter 8 that significant economic inequalities cannot be justified in this way.

[2] A point made clearly by Norman Daniels. See "Merit and Meritocracy," 210. Daniels also notes (218–19) that the meritocratic idea of procedural fairness can be paired with a wide variety of institutional justifications for positions and the rewards attached to them.

It follows from this account that if an institution is organized in a way that requires those occupying a role to have a certain ability, but could serve its purposes just as well if it were organized in a different way that did not require this ability, then equality requires that it make this change, because giving preference to candidates who have this ability is unjustified. To take an obvious example, if an institution is set up so that certain jobs require physical strength that most women lack, but would serve its purposes just as well if it were to employ mechanical aids so that strength would not be required, then excluding women because they lack this strength would be arbitrary and unjustified. Going beyond this example, it should be noted that the values that are relevant for institutional justification (the first stage of the three-stage justification I am discussing) are not limited to what might be called values of output efficiency, but include also the value, for individuals, of the opportunities for productive work that an institution provides. Determining whether an institution, organized in a particular way, is justified can thus involve trade-offs between these different values, potentially sacrificing output values for the sake of better work opportunities.[3]

This institutional account of procedural fairness also explains why selection according to ability in this institution-dependent sense is not open to the objection that it distributes rewards on a basis that is "arbitrary from a moral point of view" because the talents that are rewarded are not under a person's control, and are thus things for which the person can "claim no credit."

The idea of "arbitrariness from a moral point of view" has been widely misunderstood and often misused. As I will understand it, to say that a characteristic is arbitrary from a moral point of view is just to say that it does not, *in itself*, justify special rewards. If some characteristic is "morally arbitrary" in this sense it does not follow that it is unjust, or morally objectionable, for a distribution of benefits to track the presence of this characteristic under certain conditions, since there may be other good reasons for this to be the case.

The current use of the phrase "arbitrary from a moral point of view" derives from Rawls, who objects to what he calls the System of Natural Liberty, in which rewards are determined simply by market outcomes,

---

[3] I am grateful to Regina Schouten and Joseph Fishkin for reminding me of the need to emphasize this point.

on the grounds that it allows individuals' life prospects to be determined
by factors that are "arbitrary from a moral point of view."[4] This objection
is often understood as implying that in Rawls's view it is always objectionable for distributions to be determined by such "arbitrary" factors.
This is a mistake. As G. A. Cohen and others have pointed out, the
Difference Principle itself allows inequalities that favor those with certain
talents. So Rawls would be inconsistent if he held that it is objectionable
for differences in reward to track morally arbitrary characteristics.[5]
There is, however, no inconsistency in Rawls's position if moral arbitrariness is understood in the way I propose.[6] Under the Difference
Principle, special rewards for individuals with special talent are justified
by the fact that having such positions benefits all, that is to say, justified
by the consequences of an institution that rewards these talents.[7] Neither
the talents themselves, nor their scarcity, is taken as in itself providing
such a justification.

Let me now consider some possible objections to this institutional
justification for merit-based selection. First, this justification may seem
to depend too heavily on what the ends or aims of an institution in
question happen to be. Couldn't an institution have aims improperly
favoring, or disfavoring, some group? A state law school in the 1940s
might have argued, for example, that its purpose was to provide lawyers
who would contribute to the state's economy, and that admitting
black students would not contribute to this aim, since no law firm
would hire them.[8] This is not an objection to the view I am proposing
because the question at the first level of my three-level justification is the
normative question of whether and how it is *actually* justified to have an

---

[4] *A Theory of Justice*, section 12.

[5] G. A. Cohen, *Rescuing Justice and Equality*, 158–9.

[6] Cohen considers this alternative interpretation (*Rescuing Justice and Equality,* 166–7)
and rejects it on the grounds that Rawls needs the stronger reading of "moral arbitrariness"
as a rationale for the "benchmark of equality" in his account of how the Difference Principle
would be arrived at in the Original Position. This seems to me incorrect. As I will explain in
Chapter 9, this benchmark has quite a different basis.

[7] To complete his objection to the System of Natural Liberty Rawls would need to argue
that the mere efficiency of a practice rewarding certain scarce talents is not sufficient
justification for those who would have less under such a practice than under a more
egalitarian one.

[8] An example discussed by Ronald Dworkin in *Taking Rights Seriously*, 230.

institution involving the inequalities in question, not how such an institution is *seen as* justified.

This dependence of procedural fairness on the justification for an institution involving certain inequalities also opens up the possibility of some flexibility in the criteria of selection that are compatible with formal equality of opportunity, pushing beyond a narrow understanding of merit. For example, if there is a particular need for doctors in certain specialties, or for doctors who will serve rural communities, it would be justified for a medical school to take these factors into account in deciding whom to admit, in addition to such factors as expected scientific and clinical skill. Unlike the justification for the law school policy that I mentioned above, this justification would not be open to the objection that it is part of, and presupposes, a practice of exclusion and social inferiority.

Some policies of affirmative action for female and minority candidates may be justifiable in a similar way, and therefore compatible with formal equality of opportunity as I am understanding and defending it. Discrimination as I have defined it occurs when there are widespread beliefs about the inferiority of members of certain groups, and this leads to their being excluded from positions of authority and expertise, on grounds of their supposed unsuitability or lack of ability. Because people's beliefs about who is capable of performing well in positions of a certain kind is heavily dependent on who, in their experience, has generally done this, one important way of combatting discrimination is to place individuals from previously excluded groups into positions of authority where they can be seen to perform as well as anyone else.

Contributing to this process is therefore a legitimate aim of educational institutions that are important gateways into these professions. That is to say, no procedural unfairness is involved in giving preference to members of these groups who have the skills to perform well, provided that any loss in the promotion of the other aims of the institution is justified. Whether this is so will depend on the importance of incremental sacrifices in these aims. There are limits to the degree to which factors other than skill and reliability should be taken into account in choosing people for training as brain surgeons. But not every institutional objective has such a high marginal value. Unlike the law school policy mentioned earlier, a policy of the kind I am describing does not involve stigmatization: no group of people is systematically excluded from desirable positions on grounds of their alleged inferiority.

This rationale for affirmative action depends on the empirical claim that such a policy of preference will have the intended effect of undermining discriminatory attitudes (rather than just triggering resentment, or leading its intended beneficiaries to be seen as unqualified because they have been given this preference). It also justifies a policy of affirmative action only as a transitional measure. After a period of time it will either have had its intended effects, and will thus no longer be needed, or have been shown not to do so, in which case it cannot be justified in this way.

This example illustrates two important points. The first, mentioned earlier, is that although the requirements of non-discrimination and merit-based selection overlap, they have different moral bases. The second is that neither of these necessarily requires policies to be "color blind," or to avoid employing other "suspect classifications." Non-discrimination rules out race-based decisions only when these involve exclusion and attitudes of inferiority. Merit-based selection rules out the use of race and other "suspect classifications" only insofar as they are irrelevant to legitimate purposes of the institution in question.

Another possible objection to this institutional account of procedural fairness is that it may seem not to account for the fact that departures from merit-based selection wrong the person who is not selected. In cases of racial discrimination, one basis of the wrong to the person can be identified: being condemned as inferior on the basis of race. The argument against racial discrimination is thus grounded in the claims of individuals not to suffer this kind of wrongful treatment. By contrast, the institutional explanation of what is wrong with nepotism, or laziness in reading application folders, may seem not to capture the sense in which these practices wrong the individuals who are excluded. It makes these departures from merit-based selection seem only to wrong the institution or the employer of the selection officer. The complaint is just that this officer is failing to do his or her job properly.

The answer to this apparent objection lies in the fact that the instrumental rationale for merit-based selection is just a part of the larger three-level justification. This justification is a response to *someone's complaint* about having less than some others have. The adequacy of this response depends on an adequate defense of all three claims, including in particular the first claim that having the position to which special benefits are attached is justified to begin with. The institutional character of the rationale for merit-based selection reflects the fact that the resultant inequality is justified only if the position is administered in accordance with its justification. But this top-down step is part of an overall justification *owed to* the person who is affected. (I will offer a further response to this objection later.)

A third concern about the institutional account is that it may not cover enough cases. Suppose there are more equally qualified candidates than are needed to fill positions of the kind in question. When this is so, the institutional account might seem to provide no objection to selecting among these equally qualified candidates by preferring one's relatives, or one's former students. But it would seem objectionable if, for example, among many equally qualified candidates for a position, all of those who are selected are friends of people in power.

It is true that in such a case no one could complain that the position was being filled in a way that fails to serve the purposes that justify having it. But one could not say to those who are rejected, that these purposes would be served less well by appointing them instead. So there is no institutional justification for choosing any one of these candidates over any other.

In such a case no candidate has a claim to the position. The method of selection that I just imagined (involving favoritism for friends or political supporters of the person making the decision) is therefore not objectionable because of the result (the candidate that is chosen) but because of the way this result is arrived at. This suggests to me that the objection to this policy is that it involves a violation of the requirement of equal concern that I discussed in Chapter 2. Favoritism of the kind that seems objectionable consists precisely in giving the position to one person out of greater concern for his or her interests. If the decision in question were a private matter, to which a requirement of equal concern does not apply, then there would be no objection to "favoritism." It might be quite in order. What is needed, then, is some way of making a choice that does not involve giving greater weight to the interest of some candidate in having the position than to the comparable interest of others. This is why a lottery seems to fill the bill.[9]

---

[9] Making the choice on the basis of some other factor, such as hiring a person who is short, or wears blue shirts, would not give greater weight to the interest of any candidate. But it would not give *sufficient* weight to the interests of the rejected candidates to reject

A fourth worry is also related to the idea that the institutional account of procedural fairness is too close to an argument from efficiency. Refraining from racial discrimination does not involve giving up anything one is entitled to. But merit-based selection has costs—not only in requiring hiring or admission officers to forego preference for their friends and relatives but also a cost in the sheer labor of reading application materials carefully. So the question is: How careful must one be? How much time and effort must be put into the process of selection? The institutional rationale may suggest an answer: this must be done up to the point at which the marginal cost of a more thorough process would be greater than the marginal benefit that extra care would bring by advancing the ends that justify having the position in question.

This answer seems inadequate. Fairness to the applicants seems to require more. For example, it seems unfair to use proxies such as race, gender, or the region a candidate is from as a way of selecting among candidates, even if this would be efficient. What this suggests to me is the following. The institutional account is an essential component in an explanation of procedural fairness, because only it can explain the relevant criteria of selection. But this account leaves out the fact that, in addition to having reason to want the economic and non-economic advantages that go with certain institutional positions, people have further reason to want to be taken seriously as candidates for these positions, and considered on their (institutionally determined) merits. The use of proxies, and even the failure to read applications carefully, can involve failing to give individuals the consideration they are due (in addition to being, in some cases, objectionable for other reasons as well).

Exactly what due consideration requires is a difficult question. The answer in particular cases may well depend on the costs for the institution of exercising greater care, as well as on what is at stake for the individual applicant. My point is just that it is not settled entirely by considerations of the former sort. There is a requirement of due consideration that is independent of, and can go beyond, what is required by

---

them for such a trivial reason. (See Frances Kamm's "principle of irrelevant utilities," in *Morality, Mortality*, vol. i, 146.) Giving a job to one among several equally qualified candidates, because he or she needed it more would not, however, be open to either of the objections I have mentioned (violation of equal concern or giving weight to irrelevant factors). I am indebted to Kamm for discussion of these issues.

institutional efficiency. Like the kind of equal concern discussed in Chapter 2, this requirement seems to have both comparative and non-comparative elements. There is a level of careful consideration owed to all, although it is difficult to say exactly what this level is. Beyond this, however, it is objectionable (a violation of equal concern) if members of some groups receive more careful consideration than others.

At the beginning of this chapter I promised to provide a "moral anatomy" of equality of opportunity—to identify the various moral ideas that it involves and the relations between them. To take stock at this point, I have suggested that these ideas include, first, how the unequal positions that institutions give rise to can be justified. I have explored the possibility that the requirements of procedural fairness can be understood as corollaries of justifications of this kind. I have examined the institution-dependent idea of merit that this idea of fairness involves, and considered how the requirement of merit-based selection overlaps with but differs from the distinct idea of non-discrimination. Finally, I have suggested that this idea needs to be supplemented by a requirement of due consideration. Taken together these ideas seem to account for the requirements of procedural fairness.

This leaves open how the requirement of substantive opportunity should be understood and how this requirement is justified. I will take up these questions in the next chapter.

5

Substantive Opportunity

Procedural Fairness concerns the process through which individuals are selected for positions of advantage. The requirement I have called Substantive Opportunity concerns the education and other conditions that are necessary to become a good candidate for selection through such a process. This requirement is fulfilled if no one has a valid complaint that they were not able to compete for positions of advantage because they did not have sufficient access to conditions of this kind. The questions I will be concerned with are how this requirement should be understood and how it is to be defended.

The frequently heard claim that in America even a poor child who works hard can grow up to be rich would seem to indicate that an idea of equality of opportunity including at least some measure of substantive opportunity is widely endorsed, or at least given lip service, even by many on the right.[1] Relatively little is said, however, about the justification for this substantive requirement.

Such a justification would have to go beyond the justification for procedural fairness that I discussed in the previous chapter. As long as

---

[1] There are, however, some who reject substantive equality of opportunity. Hayek, for one, firmly rejects it, while accepting the weaker formal version of equality of opportunity, which he understands to mean the absence of discrimination and a policy of "careers open to talent." He writes, for example, that there is no more reason to object to differences in children's prospects that result from differences in family wealth than there is to object to differences that result from different genetic endowments, which children also inherit from their parents (*The Constitution of Liberty*, 94). His thought, perhaps, is that neither of these factors is under a person's control, and therefore that a child deserves no more credit for the latter (talents) than for the former. I have explained in Chapter 4 how the legitimacy of greater rewards for those with "talents" need not depend on an assumption that they deserve these rewards or can "claim credit" for their abilities. Robert Nozick also rejects equality of opportunity in this strong form (*Anarchy, State and Utopia*, 235–9). This is unsurprising, given that in his view inequalities can be justified simply by the fact that they result from the choices of individuals exercising their property rights.

there are a sufficient number of candidates who have the skills needed to make positions of advantage serve the purposes that justify them, the justification for these positions provides no reason to help more children develop the abilities to qualify for them. And even if the needs of an institution did provide reason to invest in developing a larger pool of qualified applicants, this would be a reason founded solely in the need for "human capital" rather than in a requirement of justice.[2]

A version of Substantive Opportunity as a requirement of justice is part of what Rawls calls "Fair Equality of Opportunity." He states this as follows: "those who are at the same level of talent and ability, and have the same willingness to use them, should have the same prospects of success regardless of their initial place in the social system."[3] Rawls introduces the idea of Fair Equality of Opportunity without much explicit argument, presenting it as his favored interpretation of the idea that inequalities must be "open to all."

James Buchanan endorses a requirement of substantive access to opportunity (although not *equality* of opportunity, which he believes is unrealizable) on similar grounds. When there is only "one game in town," Buchanan says, everyone must be given "a fair chance of playing."[4] Buchanan believes that differences in family circumstances are the main obstacle to everyone's having such a fair chance. To counteract this unfairness, he believes that good public education for all and limits on the intergenerational transfer of wealth should be "constitutional requirements," even if this involves some sacrifice in individual liberty and in economic efficiency.

The openness that Buchanan has in mind seems clearly to apply not only to positions for which individuals are selected through some process such as university admissions and merit-based selection for employment but also to such things as success through starting one's own business.

---

[2] Milton Friedman offers such an argument for "vocational and professional schooling." He sees expenditure on primary and secondary schooling as justified by the "neighborhood effects" of having an educated citizenry. See *Capitalism and Freedom*, chapter 6. This is a good reason for funding public education, but not the only reason.

[3] *A Theory of Justice*, 73.

[4] "Rules for a Fair Game: Contractarian Notes on Distributive Justice." Buchanan also writes, "Properly interpreted, 'equality of opportunity,' even as an ideal, must be defined as some rough and possibly immeasurable absence of major differences in the ability to produce values in whatever 'game' is most appropriate for the particular situation for the person who participates" (132).

Limits on inheritance can prevent children from richer families from having an unfair advantage in achieving the latter kind of success. But giving everyone a fair chance of playing would seem to require also that poor children have at least some initial access to capital and credit. This could be achieved through minimum inheritance for all, as proposed in different forms by Anthony Atkinson, and by Bruce Ackerman and Anne Alstott.[5]

It is an interesting question why Buchanan takes this strong position on substantive opportunity, in contrast to the views of other supporters of the free market such as Hayek and Milton Friedman. The answer, I believe, is that, unlike them,[6] Buchanan was a contractarian.[7] Like Rawls, Buchanan believed that institutions must be justifiable to everyone who is required to accept and participate in them.[8] He thought that

[5] See Atkinson, *Inequality: What can be Done?*, 169–72, and Ackerman and Alstott, *The Stakeholder Society*. Both credit the idea to Thomas Paine's *Agrarian Justice*. The case for such measures will be stronger the greater the importance attached to entrepreneurial success of this kind. John Tomasi argues that theorists such as Rawls attached too little importance to this kind of opportunity. See *Free Market Fairness*, 66, 78, 183. But Tomasi's response takes the form of constitutional protection for economic liberties rather than measures to guarantee the ability to make use of these abilities.

[6] Hayek seems to have been mainly a consequentialist, and also defended free markets on consequentialist grounds (what he calls grounds of "expediency") although he indicates that he also "takes the value of individual liberty as an indisputable ethical presupposition." See *The Constitution of Liberty*, 6.

[7] The subtitle of his article was, "Contractarian Notes on Distributive Justice." Also, in "A Hobbesian Interpretation of the Rawlsian Difference Principle," Buchanan says that he and Rawls "share quasi-Kantian, contractarian presuppositions as opposed to a Benthamite utilitarian conception" (22). And he remarks in his book with Richard Musgrave, *Public Finance and Public Choice,* that he and Musgrave are both "basically" contractarians, and that "I don't like to acknowledge that I am a utilitarian at all." For Buchanan's long and respectful intellectual correspondence with Rawls, see Sandra J. Peart and David M. Levy (eds), *The Street Porter and the Philosopher*, 397–416.

[8] There are different views about the sense in which institutions need to be justified to those who are asked to accept them. In my view, principles of morality and justice are determined by the relative strengths of the reasons some have for objecting to the burdens it involves for them and the reasons others have for objecting to alternatives that would not involve these burdens. (See *What we Owe to Each Other*, chapters 4, 5.) Buchanan's view of justification may lack this explicitly comparative character, but it is based on the reasons individuals have because of the way their interests would be affected under various principles. (See the works by Buchanan cited in n. 7.) Gerald Gaus, by contrast, holds that an institution or policy is justifiable only if every citizen has sufficient reason to prefer it to no regulation at all of the aspect of life in question. The reasons he takes to be relevant are ones based on each citizen's actual normative outlook, including his or her actual views about morality and justice, whatever these may be. Some citizens may hold minimal moral views about what they can be required to provide for others, and this leads to a

this requirement of justifiability is not met if desirable positions in the society are not "open" to all members, regardless of the family into which they are born. One cannot ask individuals to accept and abide by the rules of a "game" that they did not have a fair chance of playing.

I will begin with a question about the rationale for this requirement of openness and the range of positions to which it applies. Rawls states this requirement as a condition that must be met in order for social and economic inequalities to be just. His initial statement of his second principle of justice holds that "social and economic inequalities are to be arranged so that they are both (a) reasonably expected to be to everyone's advantage and (b) attached to offices and positions open to all" (53). The further specification "under conditions of fair equality of opportunity" is added later (72) as Rawls's favored interpretation of openness. This suggests that the requirement of openness is a condition that must be met in order for social and economic *inequalities* to be just. It would follow that the positions to which this requirement applies are just those to which unequal rewards or privileges are attached. Call this the "just inequality rationale" for the requirement of openness.

A broader and more demanding idea would be that it is a serious objection to a society if some people are barred, by discrimination or by not being born into sufficiently wealthy families, from pursuing careers for which they are qualified and which they have good reason to want to pursue, whether or not these careers are ones to which special rewards or privileges are attached. This would include, for example, such careers as being an artist or a musician. This broader requirement has considerable plausibility as a requirement of substantive opportunity: it is an objection to a society if qualified individuals have no significant chance to qualify for desirable careers requiring higher education unless they are born into a wealthy family.[9] Let me call this the "self-realization rationale" for the

---

correspondingly minimal conclusion about what the state must, or even may provide, since Gaus's requirement of unanimity gives these citizens a veto over anything more demanding. (See *The Order of Public Reason*, chapter 6, esp. 363–6.)

[9] George Sher defends a broader requirement of this kind in *Equality for Inegalitarians*. He writes (157) that "the state is obligated to render each citizen as able to live effectively as he can be" where living effectively means "embracing ends that we in fact have reason to pursue, conceiving and adopting plans to accomplish those ends, and executing the plans in ways that are efficient and flexible." As stated, this is a non-comparative requirement, and the resources it requires for different individuals will vary, depending on their ends and abilities. An element of equality enters by way of what I called in Chapter 2 the requirement

requirement of openness. I mention these two rationales because each has independent appeal, although the narrower "just inequality" rationale may be easier to defend.[10] I will be concerned most directly with this narrower requirement, although the difference between the two rationales will be relevant at some points.[11]

According to Rawls, openness requires that "those who are at the same level of talent and ability and have the same willingness to use them" should have "the same prospects of success." To clarify this idea, more needs to be said about how talent, and the motivational requirement of "effort," or "willingness," are to be understood. With these clarifications in hand, we can then turn to the question of how openness is related to equality and inequality.

As I mentioned earlier, the notion of ability that is relevant to the requirement of procedural fairness is institution-dependent. To have the ability that is a relevant basis of selection for a position of advantage is just to have those characteristics that an individual in that position needs to have in order to produce the effects that justify having that position. Similarly, the ability that is relevant to selection of individuals for academic programs that prepare people for such positions consists of just those characteristics that are needed to do well in these programs, given their aims and the way they are organized.

---

of equal concern. As Sher puts it, "the sense in which we are moral equals is that our interests are of equal importance" (94).

[10] Norman Daniels seems to appeal to the broader notion. Equality of opportunity, he says, requires that in his argument health care is a requirement of fair equality of opportunity. The availability of treatment to rectify diseases is required, he says, because diseases "impair the opportunity available to an individual relative to the *normal opportunity range* for his society." By "the normal opportunity range" he means "the array of 'life plans' reasonable persons are likely to construct for themselves" in that society, given "its stage of historical development, its level of material wealth and technological development" ("Fair Equality of Opportunity and Decent Minimums," 107).

[11] Rawls says some things that suggest the broader requirement. For example: "there should be roughly equal prospects of culture and achievement for everyone similarly motivated and endowed. The expectations of those with the same abilities and aspirations should not be affected by their social class" (*A Theory of Justice*, 63). The difference between the two rationales might be closed if the recognition accorded to "culture and achievement" is counted among the "social indicia of self-respect" that is among Rawls's primary social goods. But inequality in recognition of this kind would not have (or, I think, need) the kind of institutional justification that I am assuming is required for inequalities in other primary social goods such as income, wealth, and "powers and prerogatives of office."

Once the aims and organization of the positions and the educational programs are fixed, ability in this sense is well defined. A given individual, at a given time, either has these characteristics or does not, and some have these characteristics to a greater degree than others. But what counts as ability in this sense can change if the jobs or the educational programs are changed, and such changes will entail changes in what substantive opportunity requires. If the educational programs leading to important positions of advantage presuppose certain language or computer skills, or scientific training, then according to Rawls's conception of openness these things need to be accessible for all. If only children from rich families can acquire these skills, then children from poor families are blocked from consideration for these positions. But this reason for making such training available to all would not apply if acquiring these language or computer skills were part of the relevant courses of university training, rather than being presupposed.

All this seems clear. What is not clear is whether this institution-dependent notion of ability is adequate for understanding the requirement of substantive equality of opportunity, especially in the form of Rawls's Fair Equality of Opportunity, which requires that "those who are at the same level of talent and ability, and have the same willingness to use them, should have the same prospects of success regardless of their initial place in the social system."[12] This way of formulating equality of opportunity seems to use a notion of ability to set the standard for the kind of education and other conditions that must be available for all. A conception of ability that is to play this role cannot itself depend on some specified form of education and other developmental conditions.

Suppose, for example, that some people find abstract reasoning easy. As a result, they do particularly well in subjects such as mathematics and computer programming and therefore qualify for positions of advantage requiring these skills. This would seem to be compatible with Fair Equality of Opportunity, because those who fail to qualify for these positions do not have "the same level of ability" in these subjects as those who qualify. But this conclusion presupposes a particular form of education. Suppose we discover that there are methods of early intervention, whether in the form of special classes, drugs, or some other kind

---

[12] This problem is raised by Joseph Fishkin in *Bottlenecks*. See esp. chapter 2. I am much indebted to Fishkin's discussion.

of therapy that would enable other children to develop this same level of facility in abstract reasoning. Could we still say that the educational process I first described met the requirements of fair equality of opportunity, because those children who succeed in it are "at a higher level of ability" in abstract reasoning than those who do not? This would not seem to be the case. If, for example, wealthy families provide their children with special classes or other forms of intervention that overcome their initial deficiencies in abstract reasoning, but children from poor families do not receive these benefits, then the idea of equality of opportunity expressed in Rawls's formula would seem not to be fulfilled.

The conclusion is that, insofar as the idea of ability is institution-dependent, any judgment that two people "are at the same level of ability" will presuppose some specified form of education and other conditions in which these abilities are exercised. The idea of giving those with equal talent equal prospects of success therefore cannot be used to specify the forms of education and other conditions that equality of opportunity requires. This problem might be avoided by employing a notion of ability that does not have this institution-dependent character. But it does not seem to me that there is such a notion that is relevant to the justification of economic institutions.[13]

An alternative way of understanding Rawls's idea would interpret it simply as demanding that children's possibilities of success not depend on their families' wealth and income. This way of viewing the matter would let the education that the rich can provide set the standard of education relative to which the idea of "equal level of ability" is determined. It would hold that two children are "at the same level of ability" if, given sufficient motivation (a factor to which I will return), they would

---

[13] Fishkin argues forcefully that there is not. See *Bottlenecks*, chapter 2. The same point applies to the notion of *disability*. A characteristic is a disability in a morally significant sense if it makes those who have it less able to function in the ways they have reason to want in a society of the kind in which they live. There may be a notion of disability, such as "lack of functioning that is normal for the species," that is not institution-dependent and dependent in this way on the nature of a given society. But such a notion is not, I would argue, morally significant. The fact that a person lacks a characteristic that is typical of his or her species is morally significant only if it interferes in some way with something the person has reason to care about. It follows from the institution-dependent and socially dependent character of disability that it will in principle be possible to prevent the unequal opportunities arising from a disability either by changing society so that the relevant characteristic is not required for significant social roles or by making it possible for individuals to avoid having this characteristic.

do equally well when provided with the best education and other developmental conditions currently available.

This sets a high standard, and I will return to the problem of achieving it in a society in which there is significant economic inequality. But providing sufficiently good conditions of development for all children is difficult not only because of poverty but also because of differences in family attitudes and values.[14] We can see this problem by considering the question of "willingness," which I set aside earlier.

There is an ambiguity on this point in Rawls's formulation of the idea of Fair Equality of Opportunity. He first says that "those who are at the same level of talent and ability, *and have the same willingness to use them,* should have the same prospects of success regardless of their initial place in the social system" (my emphasis). But he goes on to state a stronger condition, that Fair Equality of Opportunity is not achieved if, due to unfortunate family circumstances, many people develop psychologically in such a way that they "fail to make an effort" and therefore fail to qualify for advantages for which they have the talent to qualify.[15] This latter, stronger claim seems clearly correct. Mere lack of "willingness," or failure to try, does not settle the matter.

There is a danger here of slipping into a kind of moralism, which is one of the serious pitfalls of the idea of equality of opportunity.[16] The phrase "equal willingness" may suggest that the requirement of substantive opportunity is fulfilled whenever we can say (truly) to a disappointed claimant, "You could have had this benefit if you had tried harder. So it is your fault that you do not have this benefit." This is moralistic because it holds that inequalities can be justified on the grounds that they are due to moral failings on the part of those who have less. An idea of desert can also make illicit appearance at this point, in the form of the idea that those who have tried hard are properly rewarded for their effort, and that those who have not tried hard deserve to suffer for their sloth.

---

[14] Although differences in economic class and differences in attitudes transmitted to children are of course not independent. See Annette Lareau, *Unequal Childhoods,* on how strategies of child rearing in middle-class families differ from those in working-class or poor families in ways that transmit differential advantages to children.

[15] The passage in which Rawls remarks that "willingness to make an effort" depends on "happy family and social circumstances" is representative. See *A Theory of Justice,* 64.

[16] Samuel Scheffler makes this point in "Choice, Circumstance, and the Value of Equality," 220ff.

Inviting as they may be, moralism and appeals to desert of this kind are both mistaken.[17] In order to see why they are mistaken we need to look more carefully at the ways in which it can be morally significant that an outcome resulted from a person's choice or is one that a person could have avoided by choosing appropriately. One way that this can be so is when what is at issue is the moral appraisal of the agent or of the way he or she acted. If a person did something "willingly" this indicates that, given her beliefs about the action and its consequences, she took it to be something worth doing. For example, if I told you I would pick you up at the airport, but fail to do this because I want to see my favorite movie star on television, this indicates something about the relative importance I assign to this pleasure as compared with your convenience and the assurance I had given you. The fact that I made this choice is thus relevant to your assessment of me and of our relationship.

But, as I will argue in Chapter 8, unequal distribution of social benefits is not justified by differences in the moral character of the recipients. So the reason why an individual's voluntary choices can make a difference to whether unequal outcomes are justified cannot be that such choices reveal the person's moral character. A different explanation is needed.

A better explanation runs as follows.[18] Individuals generally have good reason to want what happens to them to be affected by the choices they make under appropriate conditions. One reason is that their choices under good conditions (for example, when they are well-informed about the alternatives and able to think clearly about them) are likely to reflect their values and preferences, so the outcomes they choose under those conditions will be more likely to be ones that they will like and approve of. A second reason is that outcomes that result from their choices have a different meaning than outcomes determined in some other way. Gifts, for example, derive an important aspect of their significance from the fact (when it is a fact) that they reflect the donor's feelings for the recipient, and the same is true of choices we make about our own lives, such as the choice of a career.

These reasons for wanting to have a choice about important aspects of our lives depend on the conditions under which these choices will be

---

[17] I will argue against such appeals to desert in Chapter 8.

[18] I explain this account more fully in "The Significance of Choice," and in chapter 6 of *What we Owe to Each Other*.

made. The value of having a choice is undermined when one is uninformed about the nature of the alternatives, or when conditions make it unlikely that one will consider certain valuable alternatives or take them seriously. So one thing that individuals have strong reason to want is to have what happens to them depend on how they react when given the choice under sufficiently good conditions for making such choices. This is particularly true in the case of important features of their lives, such as what careers they will pursue.

An individual who fails to qualify for a benefit because he or she failed to choose appropriately under sufficiently good conditions may thus "have no complaint" about not having that benefit. Such an individual has no complaint against the institutions that provide this benefit simply because they have done enough to make the benefit available. But this is true only when the conditions under which the person made the choice were sufficiently good.

I believe that the idea behind Rawls's reference to "willingness" should be understood in this way. When Rawls writes that "those who are at the same level of talent and ability, *and have the same willingness to use them,* should have the same prospects of success regardless of their initial place in the social system," this implies that, in some cases, the fact that some people were not "willing" to develop their talents means that they have no complaint about their lack of success in attaining desirable positions. But this is so only if (and because) the conditions under which they chose not to develop their talents were sufficiently good. So in such a case this (partial) justification for the fact that some have less than they would have liked is not a claim about their moral character—that they have not put forth the effort that would make them deserve reward.[19] It is rather a claim about what *others*, including basic social institutions, have done for these people: *because* others have done enough to put them in good conditions for making the choice they *therefore* have no complaint.[20]

---

[19] Only a partial justification because it is also necessary that the institutions generating the inequality in question should be justified—that the first level of my three-level justification should be fulfilled.

[20] Sher's requirement that each citizen be given access to the means of living effectively incorporates a similar, perhaps even stronger, idea of willingness. He requires that citizens be placed in good conditions to decide what ends to adopt (*Equality for Inegalitarians*, 157) and also that "to avoid making it unreasonable for those at the bottom to try, the state must provide each with access to a package of resources and opportunities that affords him a reasonable chance of succeeding if he does try" (150).

What matters on this account is a person's *having* a choice, under sufficiently good conditions, rather than her consciously *making* a choice. It can be enough that a person was placed in (good enough) conditions under which she could have gotten a certain outcome by choosing appropriately even if, because she failed to pay attention to the fact that she had this choice, she passed up the option without choosing to do so.[21]

This view does not involve denying that individuals, particularly those growing up under poor conditions, are moral agents who are responsible for the choices they make.[22] This is so for two reasons. First, this view holds that individuals are not entitled to good outcomes: there are limits to the conditions we must provide, and after that it is up to them—their responsibility—to make their own way. Second, even if we have not done enough for people who grow up in poor family and social conditions, they are still responsible agents who may be open to moral criticism for not trying harder. As I have argued, the question of whether the choices they make reflect attitudes that are open to moral criticism is distinct from the question of whether social institutions that placed them in circumstances in which they are likely to develop such attitudes are themselves open to moral criticism, as unjust, because they do not meet the requirement of substantive opportunity. The failure to distinguish these two questions is what leads to moralism of the kind I am objecting to.

The difficulty of providing sufficiently good conditions for children to choose to develop their talents is not due only to poverty and its consequences. It also arises in cases in which the factors at work are not economic, or not purely economic, but cultural. What people are likely to develop the "willingness to make an effort" to do depends on what they see as a real possibility for them, and on what they come to value, and these things will be different for people growing up in different communities. Children growing up in communities as different as the Old Order Amish and the Roma, for example, may typically develop a "willingness to make an effort" for some purposes, but not for accomplishments of

---

[21] For more discussion, see my "Responsibility and the Value of Choice." The role that choice plays in the account I am offering is thus different from its role in luck egalitarian views, according to which departures from equality are justifiable if they result from choices that individuals actually make. For criticism of luck egalitarian views, see Sher, *Equality for Inegalitarians*, 29–34.

[22] As charged, for example, by Nozick. See *Anarchy, State, and Utopia*, 214.

the kind that society rewards most highly. This may be so because, due to the attitudes prevailing in the community in which they grow up, they do not see these accomplishments as valuable, or do not see these pursuits as real possibilities for them. And, to take a less extreme but all too familiar example, the requirements of substantive opportunity are not satisfied if young women fail to strive for positions for which they would be qualified because their families believe, and encourage them to believe, that these careers are not appropriate for women.

Attitudes prevalent in the larger society in which children live are relevant here as well as the values of their particular families. This is familiar as a negative consideration: one objection (not the only one) to racist and sexist attitudes in a society is that they undermine equality of opportunity by discouraging members of these groups from thinking of various worthwhile careers as appropriate for them. But societal attitudes can be significant in a more positive way. There may be little we can do, consistent with the rights of parents, to make it the case that every child's home environment provides "good conditions" for forming ideas about what kind of life and career to pursue. But one thing that a society can provide is a larger environment in which various alternatives are available for consideration, and presented as possible options for any child.[23] This may be the best one can do.

If procedural fairness and substantive opportunity as I have described them were fulfilled—if positions were "open to all" in the sense we have been discussing—then whether an individual achieved a position to which special advantages are attached would depend on that person's ability, understood in the institution-dependent sense, and on whether he or she chose to strive for this position in the necessary way. One should not infer from this, however, that on my view (or, I believe, on Rawls's view) talent, or ability, and willingness to develop one's ability, are personal characteristics that it is just or appropriate to reward.[24] They

---

[23] Joseph Fishkin makes this point, emphasizing that one condition of equality of opportunity (what he calls "opportunity pluralism") is a society in which a plurality of values is represented. See *Bottlenecks*, 132–7. This might have seemed surprising: the desirability of a pluralistic society might seem quite separate from the idea of equality of opportunity. The interpretation just offered of Rawls's "willingness" condition explains why there would be a connection between the two.

[24] Fishkin suggests something like this. See *Bottlenecks*, 31.

are both factors that can affect the justice of a distribution. But they have this normative effect for very different reasons.

"Talent" derives its significance from the justification for having certain positions of advantage in the first place, and its role as the basis of procedural fairness follows from this. Insofar as motivation—a tendency to work hard at a given job—is one of the qualities needed for being productive, this characteristic is an institutionally justified ground for selection, like other forms of talent. Beyond this, as I have argued, "willingness" to develop one's talents is not a positive characteristic of an individual that, in itself, merits reward. Its relevance lies rather in the fact that a *lack* of willingness—a failure to take advantage of opportunities one has to develop one's talent—can undermine a person's objection to not having certain benefits.[25] But it has this undermining effect only in cases in which we have done enough for a person by placing him in sufficiently good conditions for attaining a greater reward by choosing appropriately.[26]

This completes my clarification of the idea of openness. A career is not open to a person in the required sense if he or she is not placed in good enough conditions to decide whether to pursue that career or if he or she does not have access to the education required to develop the abilities required for that career, should he or she have them (where "having an ability" is understood in the institution-dependent sense that I have discussed). I now turn to the relation between openness and equality.

Does Substantive Opportunity, understood as a requirement of openness, require a kind of equality, or only the fulfillment of certain conditions to a sufficient degree? The latter may seem to be true insofar as what openness requires is just access to *sufficiently* good education for developing one's talents and *sufficiently* good conditions for choosing what talents to develop. Rawls's requirement that those with the same ability and the same willingness to develop it should have "the same chance" of attaining positions of advantage whatever part of society they are born into might be interpreted to mean that access to sufficiently

---

[25] I discuss other ways in which effort may seem to justify greater reward in Chapter 8.

[26] This "value of choice" analysis of the significance of "willingness to try" also explains Fishkin's objections to "starting gate" systems and to what he calls a "big test society" in which children are sorted irrevocably into different education and career tracks based on their performance at an early age. Most children at that age are not in sufficiently good conditions to make these important life choices. See Fishkin, *Bottlenecks*, 66–74.

good conditions for developing one's talents should not depend on one's social class.[27]

But what conditions for developing one's talents are "sufficiently good?" Recall that we are dealing with ability in the institution-dependent sense, which is dependent on some specified forms of education and other conditions through which it is developed. This means that a young child from a poor family has the ability to succeed in a university program or in some career, just in case he or she would develop the characteristics required for such success if he or she were to have the best kind of schooling currently available, that is, schooling as good (from the point of view of developing such characteristics) as the schooling that the rich can provide for their children. In respect to schooling, then, "sufficiently good" means "equally good."

Economic inequality thus can interfere with openness in either of two ways. Even if everyone has been provided with sufficiently good conditions to decide what careers to aspire to and given access to the best education, the economic status of a person's family might nonetheless make a difference to his or her chances of success because wealthier families can influence the process through which people are selected for positions of advantage, by means of bribes, connections, or other ways of rigging the system. This would mean that Procedural Fairness was being violated. I will return to this possibility.

The other way in which the economic status of families could make a difference is in the degree to which the conditions of openness themselves are fulfilled. Openness requires two kinds of conditions. First, it requires that all children be provided with the conditions of early childhood required for them to develop the cognitive abilities, such as language skills, and motivational tendencies, such as discipline and ambition, that are required for success in school and in later life. This requirement is difficult to meet, but as I have said earlier, the main obstacles to meeting it are poverty and the diversity of family values rather than inequality per se.

In regard to elementary and secondary education, however, inequality is a serious problem, if schools available to children of the well-to-do are

---

[27] As he also writes, "there should be roughly equal prospects of culture and achievement for everyone similarly motivated and endowed. The expectations of those with the same abilities and aspirations should not be affected by their social class" (A Theory of Justice, 63).

far better than those available to children from poorer families, enabling these children to dominate the competition for places in higher education and subsequent careers. This means that openness is violated if there are poor children who would have been equally strong candidates for positions of advantage if they had had the kind of education available to the rich, but were not such candidates because they did not in fact have this education. (These children would have ability in the relevant institution-dependent sense.)

This requirement of openness could be met by improving public education. But that is difficult to do, given the cost and what may be the shortage of supply of qualified schools and teachers. Moreover, there is the risk of a kind of educational arms race, in which richer parents keep upping the level required by giving their children more advanced placement courses and other forms of educational experience that make them better candidates for places in higher education.

It therefore may seem that to ensure that desirable positions are open to children from poorer families in a significant sense the state must either continuously raise the level of education and conditions of early development for all children, in order to meet whatever the richest families provide for their children, or else place a limit on the kind of educational advantages that rich parents can provide. This presents a dilemma, since the former seems very difficult, the latter unacceptable.[28]

It is worth considering, however, whether more of this difficulty than is commonly recognized may lie in achieving *procedural* fairness. As I have argued, the appropriate criteria of selection for jobs to which advantages are attached depend on the justifying aims of those positions and on what people in those jobs do to promote those aims. Suppose, for purposes of discussion, that these positions are justified, and that candidates are selected for these positions on grounds of (institution-dependent) ability to function well in these positions. Similarly, suppose that the appropriate criteria of selection for education that prepares people for such jobs depend on the way in which these educational programs are organized—on what skills they presuppose as opposed to those that they provide opportunities to acquire.

---

[28] One of Hayek's objections to equality of opportunity is that it would call for such measures. See *The Constitution of Liberty*, 91–3.

Given the aims of such a program, and the way it is organized, procedural fairness is violated if a selection process for the program depends in part on skills that are irrelevant to the promotion of these aims. This violation would be particularly objectionable if the skills in question were ones that only the rich have the opportunity to acquire, but it would be procedurally unfair even without this link with economic status.

If some skill, such as the ability to use a certain computer programming language, is relevant to an educational program, it might be feasible either to presuppose this skill, as something that qualified applicants should already have, or to include the training in this skill as part of the educational program itself. Suppose that this is so, and that such training is available as part of the program. Suppose also that, comparing candidates that already have this training with those who do not, it is possible to judge which are likely to do better in the program. That is, suppose it is possible to assess them on the basis of their institution-dependent abilities other than this particular computer programming skill. If this is so, then it would be a violation of procedural fairness to prefer the applicant who already had this skill over the one who did not already have it but could be predicted to do just as well in the program while acquiring the skill at the same time. This would be true especially, but not only, if the skill were one that applicants from well-to-do families were much more able to acquire.

Now suppose that an educational program that had been offering training in this skill as part of its regular curriculum were to decide to cut costs and "outsource" this part of its program by requiring applicants to have already acquired this skill. This would make it more difficult for applicants from poorer families to compete for entrance. It would therefore be open to objection on grounds of fairness, at least if the training could be offered "in house" without great loss of efficiency. And if this is correct, then the same would seem to be true in the opposite direction: an institution is open to objection if it disadvantages poorer applicants by presupposing a skill that it could provide training in without great sacrifice of efficiency. There is, of course, a question of how much cost of this kind an educational program must bear in order to avoid unfairly disadvantaging some potential applicants. This seems to me a question of the same kind as the question considered earlier of how much care an institution must take in reviewing applicants in order to give applicants due consideration.

Consider the particular case of the college admission process in the U.S. One thing that richer families can do to make their children stronger candidates for admission to college is to provide such things as advance placement courses, travel abroad to learn languages, and summer programs in science and other subjects. The argument I have just made suggests that, insofar as these enrichment programs provide skills that could just as well be acquired at college itself, an admissions process that treats them as positive factors is procedurally unfair.[29] Procedural unfairness of this kind could be eliminated, or at least reduced, by assessing applicants on the basis of their performance in some fixed array of more basic courses. If this were done, then one aspect of the dilemma mentioned would be avoided: it would not be necessary either to provide pre-college training of this kind for all students or to discourage wealthier parents from providing it. Indeed parents could be encouraged to do this since having these extra skills would benefit their children without skewing the admission process in their favor. But if procedural fairness is not achieved, then providing these benefits for one's children, however irresistible it may be, is a way of gaming the system.[30]

One effect of admission policies of the kind just suggested might be to greatly increase the number of applicants who would have to be seen as

[29] Examples of this unfairness in regard to employment include tests for abilities that are not actually required for a job and giving preference to applicants who have acquired experience through unpaid internships, which only wealthier applicants can afford to take.

[30] This bears on a point made by Thomas Nagel In *Equality and Partiality*, chapter 10. Nagel observed that parents' motivation to do as well as they can for their children can be a source of inequality in two ways. Within the family, parents advance their children's prospects to varying degrees by teaching, tutoring, and helping them to develop good habits. Outside the family, parents may also be motivated to help their children to do well in the processes of selection for positions of advantage, thorough "connections" and other ways of gaming the system. The latter threat to equality, he said, can be constrained by norms prohibiting parents from seeking advantages for their children in these ways. But society relies on what parents do for their children within the family. So it needs to encourage this, rather than discouraging or limiting it as a way of promoting equality.

The division of labor I am suggesting between procedural fairness and substantive opportunity provides a slightly different way of looking at the problem Nagel describes. If Procedural Fairness were achieved, then there would be no reason to discourage parents from doing as much as they can to promote their children's education and development. But if it is not done, and the selection process is inappropriately sensitive to the extra training and polish that parents can provide, then providing these benefits for one's children would interfere with Procedural Fairness, and would need to be discouraged just as much as attempts to gain advantage for one's children through "connections."

equally well qualified. As I suggested earlier, procedural fairness might then require using a lottery to decide among these candidates.[31] The resulting reduction in the ability of well-to-do parents to ensure places for their children in elite institutions might also reduce the tendency, which I discussed in Chapter 3, to overvalue this particular kind of success, and the tendency to believe that such success should be rewarded with great economic advantages.

Providing high-quality basic education for all, and achieving procedural fairness in the process of selection for education leading to positions of advantage, would be an enormous step toward equality of opportunity. But it would not realize this goal. It would leave the difficulty created by poor conditions for many children in early childhood, and the difficulty created by differences in family values and preferences. It would, however, reduce the competitive advantage that rich families can give their children by paying for extra education. The remaining problems would be caused more by poverty and culture than by inequality.

To summarize this moral anatomy of equality of opportunity: I have viewed the idea of equality of opportunity as part of a three-level justification for inequalities:

1. *Institutional Justification*: It is justified to have an institution that generates inequalities of this kind.
2. *Procedural Fairness*: The process through which it came about that others received this advantage while the person who is complaining did not was procedurally fair.
3. *Substantive Opportunity*: There is no wrong involved in the fact that the complainant did not have the necessary qualifications or other means to do better in this process.

I argued in Chapter 4 that the requirement of Procedural Fairness— selection according to merit, or talent—is a corollary of the justification for inequalities based on the benefits that flow from having them. The relevant idea of talent is an institution-dependent notion. It consists in those qualities that the individuals filling these positions must have, *given* how those positions are organized, in order for those positions to yield the benefits that justify them. Many cases of procedural unfairness are

---

[31] Jon Elster has pointed out that many societies make wide use of lotteries to allocate scarce goods of this kind. See *Local Justice*.

also instances of wrongful discrimination, in one or another sense of that term. But the stigmatization and exclusion involved in race- and gender-based discrimination, for example, involve a distinct wrong, independent of procedural unfairness. Finally, I argued that the institutional account of procedural fairness that I have offered needs to be supplemented by a further idea of due consideration, owed to all.

In this chapter, I located the moral basis of the requirement of Substantive Opportunity in the idea that social institutions must be justifiable to all those to whom they apply. This justifiability requires that at least the positions to which special advantages are attached, and perhaps a wider range of careers individuals in that society have reason to value, must be open to all, where openness means not being excluded from these careers on grounds other than their ability in the institution-dependent sense that I have described.

I also argued that individuals' choices have moral significance of the relevant kind only when made under sufficiently good conditions. These conditions are different from the conditions required for a person to be responsible for his or her choices in the sense of responsibility that is a precondition for moral appraisal. The failure to distinguish these two forms of responsibility leads to a mistakenly moralistic understanding of equality of opportunity.

Providing people with sufficiently good conditions to make meaningful and morally significant choices about what careers to pursue is made difficult by poverty and by the diversity of families' values rather than by inequality. Under present conditions, inequality does, however, threaten the goal of making outcomes depend on individuals' talents in the institution-dependent sense rather than on their social circumstances, because the rich can always provide more for their children than is available to others. It might seem that this unfair competition can be curbed only by eliminating inequality or by limiting what the rich can provide for their children. I suggested that this difficulty might be eased, although not eliminated, if procedural fairness were actually achieved, and the criteria of selection for positions of advantage did not include unnecessary factors that give an advantage to the rich. This would put an upper bound on the kind of public education needed to provide all with a fair chance of success. As things are, however, economic inequality is a severe threat to substantive opportunity, not only because the rich can provide more for their children but also because their political influence blocks the provision of sufficiently good public education for all.[32]

I noted at the outset that equality of opportunity has something of a bad name, because it is seen as providing illicit support for inequality. Thinking about equality of opportunity is subject to a number of pitfalls, and I will conclude by remarking on some of these that have been identified in the preceding discussion. First, it is important to bear in mind that equality of opportunity, even if it is achieved, is not a justification for unequal outcomes, but only a necessary condition for inequalities that are justified in other ways to in fact be just.

Second, it is important not to imagine that equality of opportunity has been achieved, when in fact it has not. As the preceding discussion has brought out, I hope, equality of opportunity is a very demanding requirement. Even procedural fairness is very difficult to achieve, and is less fully achieved than is often assumed. But equality of opportunity requires more than procedural fairness. It also demands substantive opportunity for all.

Finally, it is important to avoid moralism of the kind I have described. It is not moralistic to feel pleased and proud that one has worked hard, or even to feel moral approval toward oneself and others who work hard, and to disapprove of others who do not. Such feelings are quite reasonable. If one has worked hard in pursuit of rewards for hard work that are promised by the institutions of one's society, it is natural to feel entitled to those rewards, and such feelings are quite legitimate as long as those institutions themselves are independently justified. What is moralistic is to believe that these institutions are justified, and complaints against them by those who have less are unjustified, *simply because* those who have less are open to moral criticism for not striving harder. This is mistaken and moralistic because, by focusing on supposed, or even real, moral faults of those who have less, it ignores the crucial question of whether these people have been placed in good enough conditions to develop their talents and to decide whether or not to do so.

The appeal of this kind of moralism is psychologically powerful and therefore politically significant. People want very much to believe that they are morally entitled to what they have earned, and they want to keep

---

[32] As I discussed in Chapter 2, and will again in Chapter 6.

as much of this as possible. The idea that the institutional process through which they have earned their income is unjust because others have not been provided with sufficiently good conditions to compete in it, and that they should pay higher taxes in order to rectify this injustice, threatens both of these interests. Moralism provides a way of escaping this conclusion, allowing people to maintain their belief in the legitimacy of their earnings without believing that they are called on to make any sacrifice. Pointing out the philosophical error involved in this line of thinking may not undermine its widespread appeal, but is worth doing nonetheless.

6

Political Fairness

It seems obvious to many that economic inequality is having harmful effects on democracy in our society. Recent research by Martin Gilens and others has seemed to support this view. Gilens takes his research to show that on issues in which well-to-do citizens and poor citizens had conflicting preferences, political outcomes were strongly related to the preferences of the well-to-do (those in the top decile) and wholly unrelated to those of the poor (those in the bottom decile).[1] The preferences of median income people, he says, had almost as little effect on political outcomes as those at the bottom. These differences in influence, he says, are associated with economic status rather than with levels of education.

Larry Bartels has reported similar findings. Studying votes of senators in three Congresses in the 1990s on minimum wage, civil rights, and budget questions, he found that these votes were correlated more strongly with the views of high-income constituents than with those of middle-income constituents and not at all with those of low-income constituents.[2] This cannot, he held, be accounted for on grounds of tendency of poor people to vote or contact representatives less than the better off. The well-off in these analyses are not just the top 1 percent. Gilens uses the top decile, and Bartels counts those with income over $60,000 in 2006 dollars as having high income.

My concern in this chapter is the normative question of why it would be objectionable if things are as Gilens and Bartels describe. Exactly what

[1] Martin Gilens, "Inequality and Democratic Responsiveness," and *Affluence and Influence*, chapters 3 and 4.

[2] Larry Bartels, "Economic Inequality and Political Representation." Subsequent research has raised some questions about Gilens's conclusions. See Peter K. Enns, "Relative Policy Support and Coincidental Representation," and Omar S. Bashir, "Testing Inferences about American Politics: A Review of the 'Oligarchy' Result." For Gilens's response, see "The Insufficiency of 'Democracy by Coincidence': A Response to Peter K. Enns."

does the fairness of political institutions require, and how might economic inequality interfere with it?

One natural response is that Gilens's and Bartels's findings indicate that the rich have much more influence over political outcomes than the poor. Rawls states a similar view. He says that the political and economic system he calls "welfare state capitalism" is unjust because it fails to prevent "a small part of society from controlling the economy, and, indirectly, political life as well."[3] Although he does suggest that inequalities of income and wealth may lead to the development of a "discouraged and depressed underclass" that "feels left out and does not participate in the public political culture," Rawls's main objection is not that citizens in welfare state capitalist societies do not vote, or participate in politics, as much as citizens of other societies.[4] His objection is rather that such a system allows a degree of inequality that undermines the "worth" of these activities for poorer citizens. He says that "the worth of the political liberties to all citizens, whatever their social or economic position, must be approximately equal, or at least sufficiently equal in the sense that everyone has a fair opportunity to hold public office and to influence the outcome of political decisions."[5]

If political outcomes are less likely to be in accord with the views, or the interests, of the poor than with those of the rich, this can indicate a number of different faults in a political system. But I will argue that only some of these faults are properly understood as problems of influence, and those that are problems of influence differ in ways that need to be distinguished. My aim in what follows will be to identify these different faults, and to consider how they may be due to economic inequality.

Rawls notes that the idea of the fair value of political liberties closely resembles his idea of fair equality of economic opportunity, and he sometimes states the former idea in a way that makes the parallel even more explicit. He says, for example, that the fair value of political liberties is achieved when "citizens similarly gifted and motivated have roughly an equal chance of influencing the government's policy and of attaining

---

[3] *Justice as Fairness*, 139.

[4] Gerald Gaus, responding to Rawls's objection, points out that there are high levels of political participation in the United States. See *The Order of Public Reason*, 515–20.

[5] *Political Liberalism*, 327.

positions of authority irrespective of their economic and social class."[6] This parallel with Fair Equality of Opportunity is imperfect, in ways I will explore. But it will serve as a useful starting point for examining the idea of political fairness, drawing on the analysis of equality of economic opportunity developed in Chapters 4 and 5.

In those chapters, I distinguished a procedural and a substantive aspect of equality of opportunity. The procedural aspect consists of institutions that define certain positions of advantage and the powers and rewards attached to them. Procedural fairness is achieved if these institutions are justified, and if they actually function in the way that their justification requires. The positions of advantage that these institutions define are justified by the consequences that flow from having them when they are filled by individuals with the right qualifications, and the mechanisms of selection are justified if they actually select individuals on the basis of these qualifications. But even if inequality-generating institutions of this kind function properly, they are justifiable only if the positions they create are open to all. This requires background conditions, such as access to the education required to develop the relevant qualifications. I referred to this as the requirement of Substantive Opportunity.

Economic inequality can thus interfere with equality of economic opportunity in either of two ways. It can interfere with procedural fairness if the rich are able to establish positions of advantage that are not justified, because they benefit only them, or if the rich are able to influence selection procedures for justified positions in ways that unjustifiably favor them or their children. Inequality can also interfere with substantive opportunity if the poor do not have access to schools or other conditions that they need in order to compete with richer candidates for positions of advantage.

Political fairness also requires both properly functioning institutions and appropriate background conditions. But the relation between the two requirements and the reasons for them differ in important ways from the case of equality of economic opportunity. As in that case, the institutions with which political fairness is concerned create positions of advantage to which special powers are attached, and define mechanisms

---

[6] *Justice as Fairness*, 46.

through which individuals are selected for these positions. But these institutions are also mechanisms for making authoritative political decisions, establishing laws and policies that citizens are required to accept and follow. These two aspects are closely related, since the powers attached to the positions of advantage that the institutions define include powers to make such decisions—to pass laws, make judicial decisions, and establish administrative regulations.

The positions of advantage that equality of economic opportunity is concerned with are, as I said, justified by the consequences that will result if they are filled by individuals with the right qualifications. This may also be true of some positions defined by political institutions, such as the position of judge, or member of the board of the Federal Reserve. This is why these positions should be filled by appointment rather than by elections, as many judgeships are in the United States, unfortunately.

Things are very different in the case of other positions such as legislator, mayor, or president. The powers attached to these positions are not justified just by the good effects that result when they are exercised by qualified individuals. Also crucial is the fact that those who exercise these powers will have been chosen by democratic election. Having these individuals exercise these powers is thus a way of governing ourselves, a way of making collective decisions about what to do—what roads to build, what schools and other benefits to provide, and how to pay for these things.[7]

The justification for these powers depends on a number of different things. First, it depends on the structure of the process through which individuals are chosen and the processes through which their powers are exercised to make authoritative decisions. In order for being elected to confer legitimacy on office holders, elections have to have the right form. Legitimacy is undermined if, for example, some citizens are excluded from voting, or their votes are diluted by partisan gerrymandering, or if some candidates for office are excluded from consideration. But there is also a limit to the powers that even a fair election can confer. So justifiable institutions must limit these powers in appropriate ways, for example to protect the rights of citizens.

---

[7] For a defense of the alternative view, according to which individuals should be selected for political office on grounds of merit, see Daniel A. Bell, *The China Model*.

Even if political institutions are structured in a way that is procedurally fair, the powers that they confer still depend on the existence of appropriate substantive background conditions. The legitimating force of election is undermined if some citizens, even though they have the rights to vote and to participate in politics in other ways, are unable to do so because they cannot afford the means required to become candidates for office, or to gain access to the public forum.

I will return to these conditions for the justifiability of political institutions, and the ways that inequality might undermine them. My present concern, however, is just with the differences between the structure of justification in this case and in the case of equality of economic opportunity. In the case of equality of economic opportunity, although positions of advantage involve opportunities for self-realization that are good for the individuals who hold these positions, they are justified mainly on the basis of what they produce rather than on the opportunities they offer to those who occupy them. Political institutions, by contrast, are justified mechanisms of collective self-government.

One consequence of this is a different relation between the justifiability of institutions and the background conditions that enable citizens to participate in them. In the economic case, the standards of procedural fairness have "top-down" or institutional rationale: individuals are to be selected for positions of advantage on the basis of qualities that are required in order for them to be productive in the way that justifies having these positions. This rationale need not extend to the requirements of substantive opportunity. If there enough qualified candidates from rich families to fill these positions, there is no institutional reason to make sure that others have a chance to become qualified. The case for substantive opportunity is a separate, "bottom-up" matter, based on the claims of individuals not to be excluded from the system. Things are quite different with regard to political institutions. Political institutions are not adequate mechanisms of democratic self-government if the lack of proper background conditions means that many citizens are unable to exercise their political rights in an effective manner. So the justification for the structural requirements of fairness of political institutions extends to a justification for providing the background conditions required for individuals to participate in these institutions.

Two further differences between political fairness and equality of economic opportunity are also worth noting. One is that broad powers to legislate allow political institutions to alter the conditions on which their own legitimacy depends. They can do this by changing their own procedures, as in the case of legislative redistricting, but also by maintaining or failing to maintain the necessary background conditions, such as access to education and to means of political participation. A second feature is that one of the reasons individuals have for valuing the right to vote and to participate in politics in other ways is that these rights are means for making it more likely that necessary background conditions are fulfilled and that political institutions operate in the ways that they need to in order to be justifiable.

Having set out these differences between equality of economic opportunity and political fairness, let me return to the question of how the requirements of political fairness should be understood. The passage I quoted from Rawls seems to suggest that the value of the political liberties for individuals should be understood in terms of their likelihood of success in using these liberties to attain their ends. I want to question whether this is the best interpretation of political fairness. To address this question clearly, it is important to distinguish different cases falling under the two kinds of success that Rawls mentions, "attaining positions of authority" and "influencing the government's policy."

The positions of advantage that Rawls is concerned with presumably include both positions such as judge, for which individuals should be chosen on the basis of substantive criteria, and elective offices for which the relevant criterion is being elected through the right kind of process. Although some candidates may be better qualified for a public office than others, it is part of the idea of democratic election that it is up to the voters to decide which candidate to prefer. They may sometimes do this badly, as we will see. But the fairness of political institutions is not called into question simply by the fact that some people are unlikely to attain elective office because, wisely or not, most people prefer other candidates.

It follows that what fairness requires in the case of elective offices cannot be defined in terms of likelihood of success, that is to say, of actually attaining office. Success in elections is a matter of persuading others to vote for one. It thus depends, crucially, on their de facto responses. No lack of the fairness of political procedures is involved if we fail to persuade our fellow citizens to support us because of the poor quality of our arguments, or even if we fail because of their closed-mindedness or irrationality when we present them with arguments that are in fact impeccable. This problem about "likelihood of success" as a criterion of fairness is not a problem specifically about equality. For the same reason, it does not seem that there is an idea of "*sufficient* likelihood of success" that political fairness requires all potential candidates to have. These points apply as well to the other case Rawls mentions, "influencing government policy," at least when this influence is exercised through the electoral process.

Taking note of this fact, Joshua Cohen suggests that what political fairness requires is not equal likelihood of success in influencing policy but rather equal *opportunity* for political influence.[8] One might put this by saying that one's likelihood of success in gaining office or influencing policy should not depend on one's economic and social class. But it makes a difference how this likelihood is explained. If the rich had greater likelihood of success in these matters because a majority of voters particularly admire rich people and trust their judgment, this would not indicate a lack of fairness in the political institutions, whatever it might indicate about the wisdom of the electorate. A lack of fairness would be indicated, however, if the rich had greater likelihood of success in attaining office or influencing government policy because their greater wealth made them much more able to run for office and participate in politics in other ways, such as by supporting other political campaigns.

I conclude from this that Cohen's point about equal opportunity for political influence should be understood as equal access to the *means* for attaining office and, more generally, influencing policy through the electoral process.[9] In a public meeting, for example, it seems that the fair value of individuals' rights to participate would be ensured by giving each person the right to use the microphone for the same number of minutes, even though this does not guarantee anyone any particular likelihood of success.

---

[8] Cohen, "Money, Politics, Political Equality," 273. The idea of equal opportunity for influence is also emphasized by Niko Kolodny in "Rule Over None II: Social Equality and the Justification of Democracy." Kolodny discusses mainly equal *formal* opportunity for influence, exercised through voting. Cohen and I are mainly concerned with what Kolodny calls "informal opportunity for influence," which he discusses near the end of his paper (332ff.).

[9] The point made in Chapter 5 about "willingness" applies here as well. Having access to a means in the relevant sense requires not only being able to use that means if one chooses to do so but also being in a good position to decide whether to do so.

This solution depends, however, on features peculiar to that particular case: that speaking during the meeting is the main means individuals have for influencing the opinions of others, and that it is feasible to allow each of them to do this for the same amount of time. These features do not carry over to the case of political influence in a large society. There is no feasible and defensible way to give each citizen access for the same length of time to the attention of all the others, or even of important officials. In addition, there are many different forms of individual action through which individuals can make their opinions known—speaking, publishing, writing blog posts, sending letters to political officials, just to mention a few. It would not be feasible to guarantee each person access to the "same amount" of activity of this kind.

An alternative would be to say that what fairness requires is that poor citizens as well as richer ones should have access to *sufficient* means to influence the course of elections. "Sufficient means" might be defined as the ability to bring one's case for election to the attention of a wide audience for their consideration. This much would seem to follow from the idea of the legitimating power of elections. The votes in an election do not actually indicate a preference for candidate A over candidate B if the voters were unaware that B was a candidate, or if they had no way of knowing what B's merits might have been.

This conception of sufficiency is too weak, however. Even if almost all voters are aware of a person's candidacy for office, aware of his or her positions on important issues, and of the merits he or she claims to have, other candidates may still prevail simply because their message is repeated more frequently, and dominates the presentation of the choice between them in the main public media. That further exposure beyond mere awareness makes a difference is supported by the enormous amounts that people, who presumably know what they are doing, are willing to spend on political campaigns, and by the fact that candidates who win elections in the United States are almost always those who have spent more on their campaigns.[10]

---

[10] Cohen writes, "In 1996, the candidate who outspent his of her opponent won 92 percent of the House races and 88 percent of the Senate races" ("Money, Politics, Political Equality," 281). As he notes, the interpretation of these facts is complicated because incumbents are more likely to win and also better fund-raisers. Cohen concludes, "Putting complexities aside, what seems undeniable is that the success of candidates depends on their fund-raising success, that the capacity to raise money depends on their performance, that

So, even if all citizens had access to *sufficient* means for advocating their views and their candidacy for office, in the minimal sense of sufficiency I have defined, richer citizens, who are able to spend more, would have significantly greater chances of success in affecting who is elected.[11] Although it is difficult to define the idea of equal means for influence, it seems clearly objectionable if the ability to spend more gives people access to greater means that make this kind of difference in political outcomes. This seems in fact the best way of understanding Rawls's remark about "equal likelihood" of success: not as a claim literally about likelihood (probability) but as a claim about access to the means for exercising political influence: that the ability to spend more on political campaigns should not give the rich a decisive advantage in influencing who is elected and influencing political outcomes more generally.

This objection is not that electoral outcomes should be settled by rational persuasion on "the issues," and that this process is distorted if some are able to spend more money repeating their message, or engaging in forms of non-rational persuasion. Features of a political system that undermine the quality of the deliberative environment are objectionable on that ground. But the present point is different. Whether the outcomes of elections depend on rational argument or are largely or entirely contests of irrational persuasion, it is objectionable if having more money to spend on advertising gives some a decisive advantage in winning elections.[12]

Why is it objectionable for the rich to have this advantage? We might say that it is objectionable because it means that poorer citizens are deprived of an opportunity that they should have to influence electoral outcomes and political decisions, and that, consequently, wealthy citizens have an unfair degree of influence over who is elected and what

---

the ability to attract support from the groups that give depends on their conduct; contributors, by providing such support, gain some measure of influence over electoral outcomes" (283).

[11] So, just as in the case of the Substantive Opportunity component of equality of opportunity, the competitive, hence comparative, nature of the procedures in question pushes an adequate conception of "sufficiency" toward equality. I argued in Chapter 5 that this effect might be constrained, if not eliminated, if the college admissions and other mechanisms of selection were indeed procedurally fair. The analogous strategy in this case would be to make political campaigns less dependent on money spent.

[12] For depressing evidence that elections are in fact determined by irrelevant factors, see Christopher Achen and Larry Bartels, *Democracy for Realists*.

policies are followed. But by itself this seems unsatisfactory. Individuals in an entrenched minority who hold unpopular views will also be unable to influence electoral outcomes, but this does not seem objectionable in the same way. Two differences are important here.

The first is that the lack of influence of entrenched minorities is a function simply of the views of the electorate, and is therefore a possibility that cannot be avoided in a system of decision by majority vote. (It is like the advantage I have mentioned that the rich might have simply because many voters admire and trust wealthier people.) Eliminating differences in opportunity for influence that arise from unequal access to the means for influencing others may be difficult, but it is not incompatible with a system of decision by majority vote and can even enhance it. Second, disagreements between rich and poor have particularly broad implications. Individuals who are in a minority on one issue are likely to be in a majority on another issue of comparable importance. (And when this is not so, entrenched minorities are more troubling.) But being on the losing side of issues on which the rich and the poor disagree, such as the level of taxation required to provide important adequate public education, affects all aspects of life. If elected officials are themselves likely to be wealthy, political decisions in general will be shaped by their distinctive experience and interests. Even leaving aside any influence by others, they are likely to be less aware of the needs of poorer citizens, and less responsive to these needs, thus making failures of equal concern and failure to fulfill non-comparative obligations more likely.

The phenomena that Gilens and Bartels describe do seem to indicate unequal opportunities for influence.[13] But in assessing the effects of economic inequality on the fairness of political institutions we should not focus only on the responsiveness of officials to the preferences of various citizens. There are also other objections to the ways in which inequality can affect the functioning of political institutions.

As I mentioned earlier, there are standards limiting what democratically elected representatives are entitled to do. Laws violating the rights of citizens, for example, are illegitimate even if they have majority backing in a system that is fair as far as its electoral procedures are concerned.

---

[13] Gilens concludes from his research that what best explains the greater influence on political outcomes is the greater amount of money that the rich spend on campaign contributions. See *Affluence and Influence*, chapter 8.

Legislators who voted for such laws would be violating norms defining their duties that a justifiable political system would have to include. Influence that led legislators to violate these norms would be objectionable, not because it was unequal influence but because of the policy it brought about. This point is general, and applies to any cases in which there are substantive standards of legislative conduct. Here are three classes of cases in which it seems that there are such standards.

First, governments have obligations to provide certain benefits to their citizens, at least up to a certain minimum level. These include such things as police protection, protection against wrongful conviction, and public services such as basic education, drinkable water, paved streets, and adequate sanitation. If legislators or other officials fail to deliver these benefits to some citizens, they are open to criticism on this account. The charge is not that officials failed to be influenced by the views or preferences of certain members of the public, but rather that they were not responsive in the way that they should have been to reasons provided by the interests of these citizens.

Second, as I argued in Chapter 2, it is objectionable if, going beyond these minimum requirements, officials provide a higher level of these benefits to some citizens than to others, without good reason for doing so. This is not objectionable because it reflects unequal influence. Rather, it is objectionable because it involves giving greater weight to the *interests* of some citizens than to the interests of others, in violation of the requirement of equal concern.

Third, there are cases, such as decisions involving military policy, or contracts for the construction of public buildings, in which legislators and other officials have duties to be guided by considerations of the public good, rather than the interests of particular citizens. Decisions that do not do this, but allocate funds in order to benefit particular individuals or particular regions, are open to criticism, for failure to be responsive to the relevant reasons.

In cases of all three of these kinds, the objections are procedural in the robust sense I defined earlier. The charge is that political institutions did not function in the way they must in order to be defensible, because officials made decisions that were not responsive to the relevant reasons. These cases are thus analogous to violations of the procedural aspect of equality of economic opportunity, in which officials in charge of hiring, or university admissions, fail to select the best-qualified applicants. (By contrast, cases in which inequality interferes with political fairness because the rich have greater opportunity to influence elections, are analogous to violations of what I called, in Chapters 4 and 5, substantive opportunity.)

In cases of violation of procedural standards of the kind I am discussing, the idea of *influence* is relevant only as an explanation of why these violations occurred, not as an explanation of why they are objectionable. They may result from campaign donors putting pressure on legislators to adopt policies favoring them, just as violations of procedural fairness in the case of equality of economic opportunity may be the result of wealthy parents seeking special consideration for their children. But the underlying objection—failure to be responsive to the relevant reasons—is the same whether the failure was due to influence of this kind or to group loyalty or to simple laziness or inattentiveness. And when the failure is due to influence of one of these kinds, this influence is objectionable simply because it leads to decisions not being made on the relevant basis, not because it is greater than the influence that others can bring to bear.

Many of the cases that Gilens and Bartels discuss appear to involve violation of standards of these kinds. The policy questions that Gilens considered include such things as "raising the minimum wage, sending U.S. troops to Haiti, requiring employers to provide health insurance, allowing gays to serve in the military, and so on."[14] Bartels's data concerned roll-call votes in the Senate about such questions as raising the minimum wage, whether the Civil Rights Act should cover discrimination in employment, and transfer of funds from defense spending to programs to aid poor people.[15] These seem to be cases in which legislative decisions should meet specific standards, including requirements of equal concern.

There are, however, policy questions to which substantive standards of the kind I have been considering do not apply. In these cases, it might be said, political decisions should reflect, and therefore should be influenced by, the preferences of the citizenry, and it is objectionable if the preferences of some are given much greater weight than the preferences of others. There is bound, for example, to be disagreement about what promotes the common good, and in deciding what projects are justified on this ground legislators should be responsive to the views of those

---

[14] Gilens, "Inequality and Democratic Responsiveness," 781.
[15] Bartels, "Economic Inequality and Political Representation," 263.

whom they represent. What is objectionable on the grounds I have been discussing is for legislators to favor policies that benefit particular individuals rather than those that promote this conception of the good.

Similarly, I suggested in Chapter 2 that there might be various levels at which some public benefit, such as street paving, could be provided without objection. Once a policy about this level is chosen, it would be a violation of equal concern if the streets in richer neighborhoods, or in the neighborhoods of friends of the mayor, are paved more frequently. But perhaps the poorer people in a town would prefer to get by with less frequent street repairs in order to have lower taxes, while richer residents, having more disposable income, would prefer to have better streets. If, perhaps because they themselves are rich, or because the rich contribute more to their campaigns, members of the town council ignore the preferences of poorer citizens and vote to increase the budget for street repaving, this might violate a requirement of responsiveness to citizens' preferences even though (since everyone's streets are maintained at the same level) it does not violate equal concern with regard to the provision of this particular benefit.

The question of which decisions are of this type is a question in the ethics of representation—the traditional issue of when representatives should act as "trustees," exercising their own best judgment, and when they should act as "delegates" expressing the views of their constituents. For current purposes, I can leave the answer to this question open. My present point is just that if, in cases where they should act as "delegates," legislators consistently disregard the preferences of some citizens, this is objectionable, just as in the other cases I have mentioned, because these officials are failing to be responsive to the reasons that they should be responsive to, in this case to reasons provided by the views or preferences of their constituents. The primary basis of this criticism is the responsiveness of legislators to the relevant reasons, rather than the ability of voters to influence them.

Citizens should, however, be able to use the power of their votes to protect themselves against having their interests unfairly neglected.[16]

---

[16] This is what Beitz calls citizens' interest in equitable treatment. See *Political Equality*, esp. 110–13. Here there is an important difference between political fairness and equality of opportunity. It is not part of having equality of economic opportunity that one should have the means to ensure the fairness of the institutions one must deal with.

New York City Mayor John Lindsay famously lost the Republican nomination for reelection as mayor largely because of the anger of residents of the Borough of Queens over inadequate snow plowing after a blizzard in the winter of 1969. Lindsay narrowly won reelection as an Independent, but the lesson has no doubt had an impact on the thinking of his successors, and mayors elsewhere.

If one group of citizens has less opportunity to influence political outcomes than other groups do, this puts them at risk, since they are less able to protect themselves in this way. But whether the influence exercised by the residents of Queens was legitimate or excessive depends on whether what they were using their electoral power to demand was equitable treatment or special treatment, rather than on a comparison of their influence with the influence that residents of other boroughs had, should they have chosen to exercise it. One might hope that, if all have equal opportunity for political influence, their various abilities to influence outcomes would balance out, producing equitable results. But this need not be not so. The fact that all citizens have equal opportunity to influence political outcomes would not guarantee that none of them would be subject to treatment that violates the requirement of equal concern or violates specific obligations such as access to adequate education.

The example of school funding, discussed in Chapter 2, illustrates this point. As I mentioned there, state legislatures in New Jersey, and more recently in Kansas, have refused to vote for the funding needed to provide constitutionally required levels of schooling in poorer school districts. These cases involve procedural faults of the kind I have just discussed, failures to fulfill non-comparative obligations to provide adequate schooling and to abide by norms of equal concern. They are also, obviously, cases in which the poor have been unable to use their political rights to protect themselves against this kind of unjust treatment, and have been unable to do this over a long period of time.[17] This inability may be due to unfairness in the electoral system, such as partisan gerrymandering, and to the excessive power of governors in New Jersey to exercise a line-item veto.[18] But given the very widespread

---

[17] The New Jersey Supreme Court intervened in the matter in 1973, and presumably the problems of underfunding go back much farther even than that.

[18] Gerrymandering may have played some role in the New Jersey case. Legislative redistricting after the 2000 census was more favorable to minority groups than in the

opposition to raising taxes, it is quite possible that residents of poorer districts would be unable to protect themselves against unfair treatment of this kind even if their opportunities for influence were no less than the opportunities of other groups. To provide such protection something further is needed. Constitutional requirements backed by judicial review are one obvious possibility, but the New Jersey cases illustrate the limited effectiveness of this strategy.

This case illustrates another way in which inequality can interfere with the proper functioning of political institutions, even if not with the fairness of their electoral procedures. If the poor need additional public provision of certain important services, but many more people are rich enough not to have this need, it will be difficult to ensure adequate political support for providing these services to all. So, while lack of equal opportunity for influence puts a group at risk of unfair treatment, the case for having the ability to protect oneself against such treatment has a different basis than the case for having equal opportunity for influence.

I argued earlier that the proper functioning of political institutions depends on officials adhering to standards of conduct, such as the requirement of equal concern, that go beyond responsiveness to the preferences of those who elected them. Political influence can be objectionable because it is used to induce officials to violate these standards, not simply because it is greater than the influence that others have the opportunity to exercise. The present point about the case of school funding illustrates the fact that this applies also to voters. There are standards (again including equal concern) that apply to the office of citizen, and political institutions will not function properly unless citizens exercise their powers of office in accord with these standards. It is not enough that they have equal votes, or even equal opportunity for political influence.

---

decades preceding or following that. (Larry Bartels, who served on the redistricting commission in 2001, said of the redistricting plan adopted: "It's one that I think will give New Jerseyans a fair chance to tell their legislators what they think of them." *Philadelphia Inquirer*, Apr. 13, 2001.) After this plan went into effect, the New Jersey legislature adopted, in 2008, the first school funding bill to be approved by the New Jersey Supreme Court as meeting constitutional requirements of "thorough and effective" schooling for all children, provided that certain conditions were fulfilled. This bill was, however, never fully implemented, due to the election of a new governor in 2010. Redistricting after the 2010 census again reduced the power of poorer districts.

I want now to look more closely at the ways in which economic inequality can affect various citizens' opportunities for influence on political outcomes. Here we need to consider not only the means of leverage that citizens have for influencing political outcomes, such as by mounting political campaigns or contributing to the campaigns of other candidates, but also the conditions that are necessary for citizens to make good use of the leverage at their disposal. All of these factors affect what Rawls calls the "value" or "worth" of the various political liberties.

In the case of the right to vote, it is fairly easy to state some of the background conditions that are needed in order for this right to have its full value. First, there is the education needed to understand political questions and to think clearly about them. Even more clearly than in the case of equality of economic opportunity, this is a matter of having *sufficiently good* education rather than, necessarily, equal education. It is thus most directly threatened not by inequality in itself but by poverty, and inadequate provision of free public education. Inequality is a threat primarily because, as I mentioned in discussing the New Jersey school funding cases, richer members of society become less willing to pay for good public education for all.

Second, the value of the right to vote depends on access to the information that is needed in order to make informed decisions about how to vote. Since one central purpose of having a vote is to be able to express judgments about governmental policies and the performance of government officials, one kind of information that is particularly important for the value of right to vote is information about what the government has in fact done, and about the likely consequences of different policies. In a large, complex society, individuals cannot collect information of this kind for themselves. Its availability depends on institutions, including institutions such as universities and think tanks, to gather such information and, crucially, a free press and other public media to disseminate it.

The worth of the right to vote is thus threatened if the government has broad legal power to regulate what can be said or published. But even in the absence of legal powers to restrict the flow of information, the value of this right would be threatened if the only newspapers and broadcasting companies or, more generally, the only effective institutions for the widespread dissemination of information, were owned or controlled by the government. It is possible that government-owned media might operate in an open and unbiased fashion. The British Broadcasting Corporation appears to have done as well in this regard as any privately owned media company, for many years. But this depended on a tradition of government restraint and a robust culture of journalistic professionalism that cannot be counted on, given the interest that government officials have in retaining their power and shielding themselves against criticism. So government ownership of the means of communication is a risky bet.

Control of the means of communication in a country by a single private individual or consortium of individuals represents a similar threat. Again, it is possible that private owners might operate these institutions in an open and unbiased manner, serving well citizens' need for information. But this is not likely. Private owners might lack a consistent motive to shield the government from criticism and embarrassment. But a private owner or owners would still have a distinctive set of interests in economic and political matters, which they would have every reason to protect. Because the basis of the threat lies in the control of the main institutions of communication by agents representing a distinct set of interests, the threat remains even if these institutions are controlled by multiple owners who share particular economic interests. Insofar as they are in competition for market share, these owners would have some incentive to distinguish themselves from the others. But as members of the wealthiest segment of the society, they would also have important interests in common. This is thus an important way in which economic inequality can undermine the worth of political liberties, in this case the right to vote. The problem, however, lies not with an unequal distribution per se but only with unequal wealth that can be translated into power of a specific kind. But, as we have learned, this translation is difficult to prevent.

In order to decide how to vote, citizens not only need access to information; they also need access to the opinions and intentions of other potential voters. Learning what others think is crucial to making up one's own mind, and, in addition, in order to plan what to do one needs to coordinate one's actions with others. The residents of Queens who were unhappy about inadequate snow removal could form themselves into an effective group because they were neighbors. But in a large society citizens with common interests need some other way of communicating. They need both to learn what others think and intend and to have ways of coordinating their activities and presenting a united position about how they will vote. Political parties and other interest group organizations provide important ways of doing this. So the value of the right to vote is enhanced by the existence of such organizations, and by laws and other conditions that make it easier to form them, and this value is undermined by laws and policies that make this more difficult.

I turn now to the right to speak on political questions, and the right to run for elective office, for which this is an important means. The value of these rights depends on the ability to bring one's ideas, or one's candidacy for office, to the attention of a wide audience in an effective way. I have already discussed the ways in which inequality can interfere with this ability, because the rich control the main means of expression, because the poor cannot afford access to these means, or because the rich can afford so much more access that the messages of poorer citizens are "drowned out" and do not get an effective hearing.

There are many strategies for mitigating these effects of inequality, including limiting the scale of ownership of media companies in order to increase competition, providing public media to reduce the cost of access, providing public funding for political campaigns, and limiting the amount that richer candidates can spend. I cannot explore here the vast empirical literature on this topic, but will only observe that mitigating these problems has proved difficult given a high level of economic inequality.[19]

Unequal access to means of expression threatens the value of the rights to speak and to run for office and the value of the right to vote in parallel ways. If only the rich have effective access to main means of public expression, this means that poorer citizens do not have the role in politics, and in the cultural life of their society, that they have reason to want. But it has objectionable consequences for others as well. By narrowing the range of viewpoints represented in public discourse it puts everyone in a less good position to decide what policies to favor, and thereby undermines the value for everyone of the right to vote. An analysis that looks simply at the degree to which political outcomes match the preferences of rich and poor citizens, taking these preferences

[19] The nature of the problem, and possible solutions to it, also depend on the forms of communication that are in question. It is difficult to say how both may change with changes in technology.

as given, is thus too narrow as a way of understanding the possible effects of inequality on political fairness.

This illustrates how the "values" of various political liberties are interrelated. The value, for one person, of the right to vote depends on that person's access to relevant information and to the views of others, which depends in turn on freedom of the press, and on other individuals' freedom of speech. More exactly, it depends not only on the press and other individuals having these rights, and on their having the means to exercise these rights, but also *on their actually doing so*. The last is something that no institutions can guarantee. But institutions can make this more or less likely. Particularly important in this regard are policies that promote or interfere with the formation of political parties and other associations that promote political participation.

Because of the interdependence of the political liberties, it would be misleading to focus simply on the value of these liberties for the individuals who have them, understood in terms of their ability to use these liberties to influence political outcomes. As Plato pointed out long ago, the ability to influence others is worthless unless one is in a good position to decide what one should influence them to do.[20]

This point—the importance of considering not only the interests of right-holders but also of those affected by the exercise of these rights— applies not only to the value of the political rights and liberties but also to the proper understanding of the content of the rights themselves. The right of freedom of expression, for example, limits the powers of governments to regulate and restrict expression. These limits are justified on the grounds that they are necessary in order to protect important interests. So in order to decide whether a proposed regulation would violate freedom of expression one needs to determine whether it involves a power that would threaten these interests. The interests in question include not only the interests of potential speakers in getting their ideas before the public but also the interest of potential audiences, especially voters, in having access to what others have to say.[21] For

[20] Plato, *Gorgias*, 463–9 et passim. Kolodny makes this point in "Rule Over None II," 310, 332. This also may be one reason why Rawls stresses the importance of "the best total system" of basic liberties. See *A Theory of Justice*, 2nd edn, 178–220.

[21] On some views, it is the interests of voters that are paramount. See e.g. Alexander Meiklejohn, *Political Freedom*. I have argued that the content of freedom of expression depends on the interests of would-be participants, audience members, and bystanders who

example, a time limit on speeches in a public meeting is justified not only in order to give others sufficient opportunity to have their say but also to allow everyone at the meeting to hear a broad range of opinions.

To conclude: in Chapters 4 and 5, I argued that inequality might interfere with equality of economic opportunity in either of two ways. It might interfere with the fairness of the procedures through which individuals are selected for positions of advantage and for educational opportunities leading to such positions. This occurs when, for example, richer parents influence university admissions officers, or hiring officials, to give preference to their children over better qualified applicants. Economic inequality can also interfere with substantive opportunity, if children from poor families do not have access to schools that would enable them to compete with children of the rich for good jobs, or for admission to universities.

In this chapter I have argued that inequality can interfere with political fairness in ways that are parallel to these two. It can interfere with the proper functioning of political institutions, as when richer citizens influence legislators or other officials to make decisions favoring their interests. Economic inequality can also interfere with the background conditions required for political fairness if, for example, poorer citizens are unable to afford access to effective means of expression, and are therefore less able to be successful candidates for public office. Failures of political fairness of both of these kinds have to do with influence—in the former case, the influence that the rich have over elected officials; in the latter case unequal opportunities to influence who gets elected, and more generally to influence political decisions.

This description is broadly correct. I have argued, however, that in the former case, in which legislators or other officials are influenced to make decisions that favor the interests of the rich, the fundamental objection is that these decisions violate relevant standards of official conduct. Just as in violations of procedural fairness in the case of equality of economic opportunity, influence is relevant as an explanation of why these violations occur rather than as an explanation of why they are objectionable. But richer citizens are able to exercise this kind of influence because the background conditions for political fairness are not fulfilled.

---

are affected by expression, and restrictions on it, in other ways. See my "Freedom of Expression and Categories of Expression."

Here the root problem is access to the main means of expression. Economic inequality leads to a situation in which the wealthy own and control the main means of expression, or to one in which access to these means is very expensive. As a result, the rich have much more opportunity to influence public discussion of political questions. This is a problem not only for others who wish to influence political outcomes but also for all citizens, who need to be exposed to a wider range of opinion in order to make up their minds how to vote and whom to support. In addition, because running a successful political campaign is so expensive, wealthier citizens are much more likely to get elected themselves, and will have influence over other candidates and officials who are dependent on them for contributions.

There are, as I have said, various strategies for preventing economic inequality from having these consequences. But experience indicates that this is very difficult to do once a high level of economic equality is established.

7

Equality, Liberty, and Coercion

One frequently heard objection to the pursuit of equality is that the promotion of equality involves unacceptable interference with individual liberty. Robert Nozick raised this objection vividly with his example of Wilt Chamberlain, and it has been raised by F. A. Hayek among many others.[1] But the value of liberty can also be appealed to as an argument in favor of greater equality. As I said in Chapter 1, one reason for objecting to economic inequality is that it leads to some people having an unacceptable degree of control over the lives of others. So liberty or freedom in one form or another can be appealed to on both sides of debates about equality. My aim in this chapter is to clarify these debates by examining the ideas of liberty that are at issue and the various reasons we have for caring about liberty.

An interference with a person's liberty prevents that person from doing something that he or she may want to do. So, almost by definition, an interference with liberty is something that that person would seem to have prima facie reason to object to. This may be what lies behind the idea that interference with a person's liberty requires special justification, whereas failures to interfere do not.[2] If all we know about a policy is that it involves interference with a person's liberty, then there is an obvious reason against that policy. So in order for the policy to be justified, it

---

[1] Hayek, *The Constitutions of Liberty*, 87; and "Principles of a Liberal Social Order," in *Studies in Philosophy, Politics and Economics*, 171.

[2] See e.g. Gerald Gaus's Fundamental Liberal Principle, which holds that "liberty is the moral status quo, in the sense that it requires no justification while limitations of it do" (Gaus, *Social Philosophy*, 119). See also his discussion of the presumption in favor of liberty in *The Order of Public Reason*, 340–8.

must be shown that this apparent reason does not in fact apply, or that it is overridden by some other consideration.

This does not show anything unique to liberty, however. It is also true that, if all we know about a policy is that if it is followed some people will be left very poor, and much poorer than they would be under many alternative policies, then there is, apparently, a reason against this policy, which needs to be shown not to apply or else to be overridden. But even if this need for justification is not unique to interferences with liberty, it may seem to mark a contrast with equality. As I said in Chapter 1, it is often not clear what reason there is for being concerned with equality itself—that is, with the difference between what some have and what others have—rather than, for example, being concerned to provide more for those who have less. Equality can seem to be a pointless pattern, as Nozick described it, or something that people are concerned with only out of envy.

A main theme of this book is that, although inequality is not always prima facie objectionable, there are in many cases good reasons for objecting to inequality, and we need to inquire into what these various reasons are. Similarly, in the case of liberty, there are different ways in which factors can make a person unable to do what he or she wants, and different reasons for objecting to this fact. To understand the possible conflicts between liberty and equality we need to understand the various reasons at work in each case.

I can be unable to do what I would like because I lack the necessary resources, resources that some individuals or institutions could provide, and perhaps even actively prevent me from having. I may be unable to get a job because I lack the necessary education and am unable to get this education because I cannot afford the tuition. Similarly, I may be unable to get where I want to go because I do not have a car, and I lack the money to buy or rent one.

Hayek would say that in cases of this kind I do not lack liberty but only lack the power to do what I want. To identify liberty with power of this kind would neglect what is central to it, he says, by making it the case that my liberty is always increased or decreased by an increase or decrease in my wealth. My *liberty* is interfered with, Hayek says, only when someone prevents me from doing what I want by physical constraint or coercion. This occurs, he says, when there is "such control of environment or circumstances of a person by another that, in order to avoid greater evil, he is forced to act not according to a coherent plan of his but to serve the ends of another."[3]

This distinction between liberty and power is crucial for Hayek's defense of the position he favors. A guaranteed basic income would increase the power of many poor people to do things they have reason to do. If this counted as an increase in their liberty then this increase would need to be balanced against, and might outweigh, the interference with liberty involved in the taxes that are needed to support this policy. Hayek would reject this view of the matter. In his view taxation interferes with liberty, but guaranteed income does not increase it. It only gives people more power to get what they want.

Hayek is correct that there is something distinctively objectionable about at least many cases of coercion, and that this objectionable feature is not directly present in every case in which a person is unable to get what he or she wants because of lack of means. In the examples just mentioned, I am not prevented from getting an education or from getting where I would like to go because someone is threatening me with some sanction in order to get me to conform to his "plan" that I not do these particular things.

But my inability to get what I want in these cases does depend on coercion. My lack of money makes me unable to do what I want because getting what I want depends on having or using something that is someone else's property, and that person will permit me to have or use that thing only in exchange for money. I can't simply take a car, because all the cars around belong to people. The law forbids me from using them without the permission of the owners, and I would be subject to punishment if I did. So my lack of ability to get what I want without money depends on the existence of property rights, backed by coercion, and this will be so in all the cases in which, in Hayek's terms, my power to get what I want would be increased by an increase in my wealth.

The importance of "background coercion" of this kind was emphasized long ago by Robert Hale.[4] Hale went on to say, less plausibly, that whenever a party to an arrangement agrees to certain terms only because

---

[3] *The Constitution of Liberty*, 20–1, 133.

[4] Hale, "Coercion and Distribution in a Supposedly Non-coercive State." G. A. Cohen makes the same point in "Justice, Freedom, and Market Transactions." For discussion of Hale's view, see Barbara Fried, *The Progressive Assault on Laissez Faire*.

the other party's insistence makes this necessary, the first party is coerced into doing this. If, in the example I gave, I hand over money that I would otherwise use to buy food in order to rent the car I need to get to a job interview, Hale would say that I am coerced into making this payment. He is quick to add that this does not mean that what the rental agency does in such a case is impermissible, or that the contract I make with them is invalid because not voluntary. Whether something involves coercion in this sense, and whether it is wrong are, he says, two separate questions. But it does seem to strain common usage, and perhaps to drain the idea of coercion of much of its force, to say that every case of mutually beneficial *quid pro quo* exchange is coercive.[5]

What Hayek's distinction between liberty and power calls attention to, however, is not a distinction between coercion and other ways in which a person might be made unable to do what he or she wants, but rather a distinction between two reasons for objecting to factors that prevent one from doing what one wants to do, whether these factors amount to coercion or not. On the one hand, one has reason to object to a valued option being made unavailable, or available only at greater cost or risk. The strength of this reason depends simply on the strength of the reason for wanting to have the option in question. But there is also an independent objection to being under the control of another person and subject to his or her will in the way that Hayek describes.[6] Reasons for objecting to this vary, depending not only on the value of the options that are made less available but also on other factors, of which I will mention three.

First, reasons for objecting to being subject to another person's will depend on one's relation with that person. It may be less (or perhaps in some cases more) objectionable to be under the control of a family member, or someone one loves, than to be under the control of a stranger, or someone with whom one has a long-standing adversarial relationship.

---

[5] Although it may be that exchange is something less than ideal from a moral point of view when it is understood simply in this *quid pro quo* way. For an investigation of how exchange might lack this objectionable feature, see A. J. Julius's "The Possibility of Exchange."

[6] This reason has been emphasized by political philosophers writing in the republican tradition. See e.g. Philip Pettit's *Republicanism* and *Just Freedom*, and Quentin Skinner's *Liberty Before Liberalism*, chapter 2, esp. 84.

Second, the strength of the reasons for objecting to being under another person's control depends on the amount of discretion that this person has in deciding what to tell you to do. As Hayek observes, coercion is less objectionable when it is regulated by law.[7] This may be in part because law renders the interference more predictable, allowing one to plan in a way that takes it into account. But there is, in addition, a personal element: one stands in a different, and more objectionable, relationship to a person who can command one to do whatever he or she wishes than one does to a person who can command only in ways, and for reasons, that are set by laws that that person did not choose and cannot change. In cases of the former kind one is dependent on that person's will in a way that can be particularly objectionable.

Third, the degree to which it is objectionable to be under the control of another person also depends on the aspect of one's life that is subject to control. It is worse to have someone dictate how one will lead one's personal life—for example whom one will marry—than to have someone determine other limits on what one may do, such as how close to the edge of one's property one may build a house. One reason for this is that the meaning of many personal choices, such as the choice of a spouse, is altered, and often undermined, if it is made or strongly influenced by someone else (whether this influence is exercised through threats or through offers, such as offers of money, or a job). It is important that certain choices depend only on one's own reasons, and on reasons of a particular kind (for example, not reasons of financial gain).

The distinction Hayek draws is thus deeper than the distinction between coercion and other limits on a person's ability to get what he or she wants. This can be seen from the fact that we need to consider objections of both of the kinds I am distinguishing in order to understand what is objectionable about coercion and in order to decide when coercion can nonetheless be justified.

In most cases, coercion is subject to objections of both of these kinds. Coercion typically involves a threat—"Do A or I will do B!" where B is something that the threatened person has good reason not to want. The threat is thus something that this person has reason of the first kind

---

[7] *The Constitution of Liberty*, 21. Pettit and Skinner also emphasize that what is objectionable about unfreedom is being subject to the *arbitrary* will of another (*Republicanism*, 55–7; *Liberty Before Liberalism*, 70).

I mentioned to object to because it worsens his or her choice situation, by removing the option of refraining from doing A without suffering the threatened penalty. In addition, the threat may be objectionable because complying with it involves being under the control of the other person. Offers are often thought not to be coercive, insofar as an offer improves a person's choice situation and is therefore not subject to the first of these objections.

But offers can be objectionable in the second way. Suppose your rich uncle says he will buy you a car if you give up your plans to get married right away. You still have the option of getting married now without getting a car, and you have the new additional option of getting a car if you marry later. So it may seem that your set of options is not made worse, and perhaps improved, by your uncle's offer. (Although the significance for your life of getting married now may be altered by the fact that it involves passing up the chance to get a car, which you may need.) What makes the case seem like coercion, however, is the attempt by your uncle to control your decision whether or not to get married now. This is a kind of decision that you have particularly strong reason to want to make on your own, independent of others' control or influence.

The permissibility of coercive threats (or indeed "coercive" offers) depends on a number of factors, including at least: (1) the value of the option that is foreclosed, or made less available or attractive, and one's entitlement to engage in it; (2) the magnitude of what one will lose if one does not comply with the demand that is made; (3) the threatener's entitlement (coercion aside) to deny you this thing; and (4) the fact that complying with the demand involves being under the control of this other person in this particular way.

Consider first the standard case of a robber with a gun, who confronts you saying, "Your money or your life!" In this case there are, first, your reasons for wanting to keep your money, and for wanting to stay alive. In addition, there is the fact that, quite independently of any question about coercion, you are entitled to keep your money and the robber has no right to kill you. This seems to me enough to make what the robber is doing impermissible. There is, in addition, your reason for objecting to being under the control of the robber. It is humiliating to have to submit to such a demand. Reasons of this kind are even more important in other cases.

Consider, for example, the case of an employer, who has good economic reasons for reducing his workforce, who tells a worker that he will not fire her if she is willing to have sex with him. In this case, the worker is not entitled to continued employment and the employer (leaving aside the permissibility of coercion, which is the question at issue) has the right to fire her. The impermissibility of what the employer does is explained by the impermissibility of using his right to fire the worker to compel her to act in accord with a plan of his, in a way that is particularly objectionable because of the personal significance of the choice involved. The conclusion to draw from this is that, although for reasons of economic efficiency (and perhaps other reasons as well), employers must have the right to decide whom to hire and fire, it is impermissible for them to use this power in the way just described (or, for that matter, to use it as a way of extorting gifts or other favors from employees or potential employees).

Consider now the coercion involved in the criminal law. Criminal law raises problems of justification because the penalties it inflicts involve very serious losses—such as imprisonment, loss of property, and perhaps even loss of life—that individuals are normally entitled not to suffer. Many criminal laws nonetheless seem to be clearly justified because of the protection that these laws provide for everyone, and also because the particular forms of behavior that are sanctioned—such as murder and armed robbery—are ones that people have no good reason to engage in. The fact that being subject to such laws involves being controlled by others does not seem to be a crucial factor.

In many cases in which people have objections to laws, such as to environmental laws, zoning codes, occupational health and safety regulations, and, more to the present point, tax laws, these objections are based mainly on the value of the opportunities that are foreclosed, rather than on the fact that obeying these laws involves being controlled by some other agent. An objection of the latter kind comes to the fore most clearly in the case of laws regulating more personal forms of conduct, such as laws against drug use, or laws requiring motorcyclists to wear helmets. Here, in addition to the loss of an opportunity, there is reasonable resentment against being told "how to live one's life." And one may have reason to feel this resentment even if one does not value the opportunity in question (even if, say, one would never think of riding one's motorcycle without a helmet).

Any action or policy that is coercive in the broad sense of attaching an unwanted outcome to a course of action in order to discourage someone from acting in that way is likely to be open to prima facie objections of both of the kinds I have been discussing. To decide whether such an action or policy is permissible we need to consider, on the one hand, the reasons of both of these kinds that individuals have for wanting not to be subject to such demands and, on the other hand, the reasons for allowing such demands to be made. My present point is that the reasons that count against demands that are coercive in this broad sense are quite varied, and include reasons for wanting certain opportunities to be available (reasons for wanting what Hayek called power) as well as reasons for objecting to being controlled by another person.

With these ideas about liberty and coercion as background, let me turn now to the question of conflicts between liberty and the promotion of equality. One way of promoting equality is through redistributive taxation, which takes resources from some in order to provide benefits for others. Another way of promoting equality, or avoiding inequality, is through what has been called *predistribution*, that is to say, through the laws and policies that determine individuals' pretax incomes.[8] The main things that Rawls's Difference Principle, for example, is supposed to apply to are the aspects of an economic system that generate inequality in pretax income and wealth. Laws protecting intellectual property are a good example. Shareholders of Disney and Merck would not be as wealthy as they are today if the patents and copyrights held by those companies did not last as long as they do. Less extensive rights to intellectual property would, arguably, lead to less inequality. For reasons I will discuss, predistribution is the more fundamental question. But since redistributive taxation receives much attention I will consider it first.

Taxation may seem a prime example of interference with liberty. Paying part of one's income as taxes, when the alternative is a fine or imprisonment, leaves one less able to do things that one would want to do with the money one has to pay. In addition, taxation often involves being forced to serve the aims of another rather than one's own—to pay for wars one disapproves of, to provide benefits to others whom one believes do not deserve these benefits, or to pay for projects, such as sports stadiums or museums, that one believes to be wasteful. Being

---

[8] I take the term "predistribution," from Jacob S. Hacker, "The Institutional Foundations of Middle-Class Democracy." For earlier use, see James Robertson, "The Future of Money." Martin O'Neill and Thad Williamson discuss the concept more extensively in "The Promise of Predistribution."

required by law to pay one's rent, or to pay other debts one has incurred, would not be objectionable in this way, insofar as these debts were undertaken voluntarily, in pursuit of one's own ends, rather than forced on one by another's will.

It might be responded that we nonetheless owe these taxes, insofar as they are levied by a legitimate political and legal order that has authorized the expenditures that these taxes are used to pay for. The money that one must give up in paying taxes is, therefore, like the money one owes in rent, not money one is entitled to keep and do with as one wishes. This response might be said to be question-begging, because it assumes the legitimacy of the tax laws, which is exactly the point at issue. But the claim that one is entitled to one's pretax income also presupposes the legitimacy of the particular political and legal framework within which this pretax income was earned. Tax laws are part of that framework, and have the same legal basis as the rest of it, including laws defining property rights. So it does not make sense to claim that taxation is illegitimate because it takes away what, *according to that legal framework,* belongs to a person.[9]

The best way of understanding the objection to redistributive taxation is therefore not that it is objectionable because it takes away part of the pretax income that people have earned and are entitled to according to the particular legal system in which they live. The objection should be, rather, that a legal and political system that allows for redistributive taxation is, for that reason, unjust (and the pretax incomes earned within it are therefore to some degree also morally tainted).[10]

Any plausible view permits *some* forms of taxation, however. Suppose that some view holds, for example, that taxes to pay for law enforcement and national defense (but only such taxes) are legitimate. Laws requiring individuals to pay just these taxes, on pain of legal penalties such as fines or imprisonment, would therefore not, on this view, be counted as objectionable interferences with individual liberty. These laws would be coercive, and would diminish individuals' means to pursue their ends in one way, by reducing their disposable income, although they might

---

[9] This is the point made by Murphy and Nagel in *The Myth of Ownership*, arguing against what they call "everyday libertarianism." See esp. 31–8.

[10] Murphy and Nagel discuss this form of libertarianism, as opposed to "everyday" libertarianism, on pp. 64–6.

increase it in other ways, through the protection these taxes make possible.

The money that people would use to pay their taxes under such a system, like the money they use to pay their rent, must be *their* money— money that it would be wrong for someone else to remove from their bank account. But it is not a prima facie objection to such taxation, which needs to be overcome, that it "takes away" money that is theirs in this sense, because they are not entitled to keep this money. This is not because their right to keep the money is *overridden* by other consider- ations. One's right to keep the money needed to pay one's rent is not overridden by the claims of one's landlord. Rather, one does not have such a right because of the lease one has entered into, or, in the case of taxes, because of the (valid) tax laws that apply to one.

Generalizing from this case, I conclude that the enforcement of tax laws per se is not the issue. If one owes something, it is not an objec- tionable interference with one's liberty, or one's property rights, to be required to pay it. The question is what taxes one can legitimately be said to owe. This question, of the legitimacy of taxation in general, is a part of what I called earlier the question of predistribution—that is to say, of the legitimacy of an overall framework within which property is acquired and exchanged, and income earned. The question might be, for example, whether a system in which a person is allowed to keep only part of what he or she receives from certain transactions is justified or whether a justifiable system must allow a party to such a transaction to keep all of what the other party offers.[11]

To determine the legitimacy of the tax laws involved in an institutional framework we must consider both the justifications that might be offered for having these laws and, on the other hand, the objections to them and limitations to which they may be claimed to be subject.

Here are three possible forms that justifications for tax laws might take. Tax laws might be justified on the grounds that the political system is a legitimate way of making collective decisions to undertake projects, and that these tax laws are a fair way of raising the funds required to carry out these projects. Although I believe that tax laws can be justified

---

[11] This is another way of putting one of the main points of Murphy and Nagel's book. But *Redistribution and Predistribution* would have been a less snappy title than *The Myth of Ownership*.

in this way, I will not explore this kind of justification here, both because it requires defending a general theory of political legitimacy and because it is one in which considerations of equality are less likely to be invoked.

A second form of justification for taxation is that it is a fair way of paying for benefits that must be provided in order for the legal and political system itself, including the property laws that it involves, to be justifiable. These benefits might include, for example, education and other conditions required in order for everyone in the society to have an opportunity to participate in the economy, and conditions required for them to have an effective role in the political process. A third form of justification would argue that taxation is needed simply to reduce inequality, either because it is itself unjust or because of its harmful consequences, such as the corruption of the political system.

I have discussed arguments of the second kind in previous chapters, particularly Chapters 5 and 6. I list them here for purposes of discussion, and will mention one further argument below. But the main aim of this chapter is to consider the arguments on the other side. One such argument would be that taxation is objectionable because it is incompatible with property rights that individuals have independent of any social institution. This is not currently the most widely held view.[12] But it is worth considering why it should be appealing.

One reason for its appeal might be the thought that social institutions defining property rights are open to moral criticism. Not just any way of defining these rights could be legitimate. It may seem that this criticism must be based on rights that individuals have independent of any such institutions, and a right to property seems one obvious candidate. A second, more specific supporting reason is that one can imagine actions that are clearly wrong, quite independent of any social institutions, and seem to be wrong because they involve violation of property rights.

Suppose that a family clears some land and raises crops to survive the winter, and that they do this without wronging anyone else—leaving "enough and as good" for others, as Locke would say. If a band of armed men then come along and take the crops this is clearly wrong. To put the

---

[12] It is rejected by Hayek, *The Constitution of* Liberty, 158–9; by Friedman, *Capitalism and Freedom*, 26; and more recently by Gaus, *The Order of Public Reason*, 509. Dissenters include Nozick and Eric Mack, "The Natural Right of Property."

matter in contractualist terms, any principle that permitted such an action is one that it would be reasonable to reject.

The reasons for rejecting such a principle are the reasons that people in the position of the family have to be able to provide for themselves, and to have enough confidence in having use of certain objects in the future to make it rational to invest time and energy in making those objects usable. These reasons are sufficient grounds for rejecting a principle that would permit taking the crops because there are no comparably strong reasons for insisting on being permitted to act in this way. What the family has done left them with "enough and as good," so they had the opportunity to provide for themselves in the same way that the family has done.

The reasons for rejecting such a principle—reasons for wanting to have control over objects that are needed to provide for one's life, and in having the stable control over these possessions over time that is needed to plan, and to carry out one's projects—are among our most basic personal interests in property and are what makes rights of personal property so important.[13] So it is natural to conclude that the imagined action is wrong because it violates the property rights of the family. But this is a mistake. The wrongfulness of violating property rights differs in several ways from the "natural" wrongfulness of interference with interests that make property important.

There can be obvious natural wrongs of the kind I described because there are cases in which it is clear that the perpetrators have interfered with the victim and done this in circumstances in which they have no justification. But in many cases it is not clear what constitutes interference. Have I interfered with you if I tunnel under your land to mine ore deposits that you had no idea were there? Have I interfered with you if I dig a well near our property line to extract oil, most of which lies under your land? One thing that social institutions of property do is to define rights of control over land and other objects that serve the basic interests in property that I have listed. If established institutions do this in a defensible way, then it is wrong to violate the rights they define, whether or not this particular violation actually involves an interference with the victim's life and activities, in a sense of interference that is independent

---

[13] See Freeman, "Capitalism in the Classical and High Liberal Traditions," 31 and n. 27, and Rawls, *A Theory of Justice*, 53, 54.

of this institution. And this can be wrong whether or not the agent had, in that particular case, alternatives that offered "enough and as good."

Institutionally defined property rights also include the power to transfer—to confer on others an exclusive right to use of an object that does not depend on whether a third party's use of that object would interfere, in a sense independent of that institution, with its use by the person to whom the object is transferred. Nor does the exclusive right to use that the transferee acquires depend on the idea that there is "enough and as good" available to the person who is excluded from using that object. The transfer itself confers the right to exclude. This allows for the possibility that the main reason the person has for wanting the transferred object may be just to have the power to exclude others from its use, in order to demand a higher price from them for using it, perhaps by holding it until some later date at which greater demand or scarcity of supply causes the price to rise. Holding for future exchange is a kind of use, but it is a kind of use that is itself dependent on (rather than merely protected by) the power to exclude.

This is not to say that rights of this kind cannot be justified, but only that they are not justified by an argument from non-interference, of the kind I have been discussing. Institutions can create property rights that are justified instrumentally on grounds other than the need to protect these most basic personal interests in property. Such a justification must take into account the overall consequences of having such a system in a particular context, including its distributional effects. Intellectual property rights are an extreme example of rights of this kind, rights that are created by custom or legislation, and can then be transferred and exchanged.

If by property rights one means rights that go beyond claims to non-interference in the ways just described, and that include the power to transfer such rights to others, then all property rights depend on social institutions, in two ways: they are defined by social institutions and their justification depends on the justification for those institutions. So from the fact that there are no natural property rights it does not follow that institutions can fashion and revise property rights in any way at all without being subject to moral criticism.[14] There are limits to the ways

[14] As some critics of Murphy and Nagel's *Myth of Ownership* mistakenly interpreted the view they defend there as implying.

in which institutions can define property rights, because these rights must be justified by the way they serve, protect, and more generally are compatible with, important interests. These interests include, but go beyond, what I called our most basic personal interests in property, which as I have argued can be the basis for wrongs that are independent of any institutions.

Whether a particular system of property rights in the fully extended form I have described is justifiable, and violations of the rights it defines are therefore wrongful, depends on the effects of the system of holdings and exchange that that system creates. Such a system is justifiable if the benefits it provides are sufficiently important to make it unreasonable for people to object to being excluded by the system from access to objects and other opportunities they have reason to want.[15] Considerations of liberty, including but not limited to reasons for objecting to being told what to do by others, play a role in answering this question, along with considerations of economic efficiency. Insofar as there are reasons for objecting to inequality, because of its consequences or on other grounds, these should also have a role in this process. The justifiability of a system of rights depends on how all of these reasons balance out.

Some examples will serve to illustrate this process of justification. Consider first the case of rights to hold and exchange personal property. We have strong reason to want to be able to use, and to exclude others from using, the space in which we live and the objects that we need to carry out our lives. We need to count on being able to use, in the future, objects that we need to carry out our projects and we therefore have reason to exclude others from using these objects. Ways of defining, or redefining, property rights are open to serious moral objection if they are incompatible with these most basic reasons. This does not mean that, for any project I might have, a legal system is open to objection if it does not give me the kind of control over objects that I need in order to carry out that project. Giving me that kind of control might be incompatible with the reasons that others have to carry out *their* projects.[16]

---

[15] This general point is acknowledged by Nozick when he recognizes the need for his Lockean Proviso. See *Anarchy, State, and* Utopia, 175–82. The difference between us lies in the fact that he sees the threshold of justifiability as being so low.

[16] A point vividly illustrated by Nozick's example of choosing whom to marry, in the section on "Having a Say over What Affects You" in *Anarchy, State, and Utopia*, 268–71. Nozick is quite correct that there can be no general *right* to have a say over what affects you.

What it does mean is that a defensible system of property rights needs to define those rights in a way that is responsive to the reasons of this kind that *everyone* has. There are often different ways of doing this. And there may be ways of doing some of these things that do not involve property rights. Our reasons for wanting control over our living space might be served by a system of leasing that did not, like a property right, include the power to sell. But whatever system of laws or customs serves the role of protecting these interests, there is serious objection to changing it in ways that would make it fail to do so. And this might be so even if this change would promote economic equality in some way.[17]

Now consider, at the opposite extreme so to speak, the process of justification in the case of laws creating intellectual property rights. Patent and copyright laws forbid people from doing certain things—for example, from manufacturing and selling certain drugs, or from reproducing certain texts and images. They thus render these people less able to do what they want (decreasing what Hayek calls their power) by subjecting them to directives backed by the threat of punishment (also decreasing what Hayek called their liberty). These laws thus also decrease the power of others, who would like to take these drugs or enjoy these images, by making these things less cheaply available.

On the other side, these rights to exclude provide income for the holders of patents and copyrights, contributing to their ability to get the things they want. Making these rights more extensive (for example, by making patents and copyrights last longer, or making them apply across a wider geographical area) would make holders of these rights richer, increasing their ability to get what they want. It thus may encourage others to invent such things.

It would also increase inequality. So *if* there are reasons for avoiding or reducing this inequality (based, perhaps, on its effects), these would be reasons for making these rights less extensive. Making intellectual

But some ways of defining rights could still be open to objection because of the particular ways that they deprived some people of control over their lives. So the objection that Nozick was responding to need not be stated in terms of a general right of the kind he shows to be indefensible.

[17] This is why Rawls includes rights to hold personal property among the rights of the person that are part of his first principle of Equal Basic Liberties, which cannot be abrogated even to promote fulfillment of his Difference Principle. See Samuel Freeman, "Capitalism in the Classical and High Liberal Traditions," 19 and 31-2.

property rights less extensive would not, as far as I can see, be open to objection on the grounds that it reduced liberty, since there are considerations of liberty, of various sorts, on both sides of the question. Less extensive rights would decrease the ability of right holders to get what they want while increasing the corresponding ability of others. The degree to which people are dictated to by the state seems to be the same under either arrangement.

If anything, it appears that, even leaving questions of equality aside, considerations of liberty would *call* for making these rights less extensive. At least they do not provide an objection to doing so. The main reason for making patents and copyrights last longer is that they are needed to provide incentives to produce products that will be useful. So if there is a conflict here it is between the benefits that could be provided in this way (increases in some people's "power" to get what they want) and considerations favoring equality.

I believe that this description of the process of justification applies in general to questions about the moral limits on the definition of property rights. It is a complicated matter how this process of justification comes out in particular cases. But it seems clear at least that considerations of equality have *a* role to play, and that they are not ruled out by the fact that they sometimes conflict with considerations of liberty. A conflict between liberty and equality seems most direct in cases in which inequality is generated by particular transactions in which individuals exercise rights that they clearly must have, and in which equality can be promoted only by either restricting these transactions or taxing the income that results from them.

This is the situation in Nozick's Wilt Chamberlain example. The extra dollars that Wilt receives from his fans for the pleasure of watching him play lead to a significant increase in economic inequality. Even if this inequality is something there is reason to prevent, it cannot be prevented by forbidding what Wilt and his fans do. What good is money if one can't spend it on tickets to basketball games if that is what one wants to do? And it has to be up to Wilt whether to play for a given amount or not. So it seems that the only way to avoid this increase in inequality is to tax Wilt's earnings. What determines whether this is permissible? This is a special case of the more general question of individuals' claims to keep the full amount that they receive through various transactions. I will consider first the case of profits on the exchange of property, and then return to the case of payment for services.

Take the case of profits from the sale of one's house, since that is a case in which the personal reasons justifying of property rights are particularly strong. Individuals have strong reason to want to control the space in which they live, to be able to use it when they wish, and to exclude others from it when they wish to do so. This is among what I called earlier one of their most basic reasons for concern with property. Individuals also have strong reason to want to be able to choose where to live and to change living places if they want to do so. In the light of these reasons, a defensible system of rights must provide for individuals to have the ability to exclude others from their personal space, and must not require them to live in certain places or forbid them from moving should they wish to do so.

It remains the case that not everyone can live where they would most like. A system of property rights in housing, transferable on the market, is one obvious way of solving this problem. Such a system preserves stability of control over one's living space since people are free not to move unless they are offered a price that makes moving seem desirable to them (i.e. something that at least meets their "reserve price"). Allocating scarce housing to those who are willing to pay more for it makes sense insofar as it results in an allocation of resources that is responsive to individuals' different tastes in housing and to the different values they place on housing as compared with other goods. (At least it has this effect insofar as the marginal utility of money is roughly the same for different individuals. This may not be so when wealth and income are very unequal.)

The very strong case for exchangeable property rights in housing thus rests in part on the most basic personal reasons for concern with property, and in part on efficiency considerations of the kind just mentioned, to which one might add that such a system helps to insure an appropriate amount of housing, since if housing is scarce rising prices will attract more investment in residential construction.

The question is whether the property rights in housing that these considerations support preclude taxes on the profits from resale of one's house. It seems to me that they do not, although they place limits on what this tax could be. First, it is essential that buyers and sellers know in advance what they will pay and receive. (Reasonable expectations should be protected.) Second, it is essential that sellers receive at least their reserve price, and that buyers not be forced to pay more than the property is worth to them. Third, the efficiency properties of the market depend on its being the case that if some would-be buyers are willing to pay more then the seller would get more, even after taxes, by selling to them. Taxes therefore cannot take away all of a seller's gains beyond his or her reserve price. But it does not follow from this that the seller must be allowed to keep the full amount that the buyer pays.

What the buyer is willing to pay will depend, of course, on how much money the buyer has, but also on the availability of other housing that is just as desirable. So what I have just concluded is that the reasons supporting property rights in housing do not support the conclusion that a seller is entitled to the full scarcity premium of his or her property. Any such tax would, in Nozick's phrase, interfere with certain "capitalist acts between consenting adults" by preventing transactions in which the seller is able to keep exactly what the buyer pays. But the interests of buyers and sellers in being able to make exactly this kind of transaction seem quite weak in comparison with the other interests in property rights that I have mentioned.

This may seem unsatisfactory. A tax on real estate transactions the proceeds of which go straight into the President's personal bank account would be unacceptable, even if the limits just mentioned were observed. Moreover, such a tax would be objectionable even if it were well known in advance of any transaction and, I think, even if the law in question were enacted by a democratically elected legislature. Can what is objectionable about this be explained without appeal to the idea that sellers' property rights entitle them to the full amount of what others are willing to pay for their property? (Or, what seems less plausible, that buyers are entitled not to pay more than what the seller actually receives?)

A tax of this kind would be objectionable because, first, sellers have reason to want to keep more of what buyers are willing to give them, so some reason has to be given for their not getting this. Second, there is no good reason why sellers should receive less or buyers pay more in order for the President to benefit in this way from every transaction. So if some taxes on gains from exchange are just, it must be because, in addition to being known in advance and enacted through fair procedures, they are supported by good reasons.

The two classes of reasons that come to mind are reasons arising from the conditions required by the legitimacy of the system of property rights and exchange itself and reasons for promoting important public goods.

I will focus on reasons of the former kind, because the taxes they support are the most likely to be redistributive and because this is where considerations of equality are most likely to play a role. In order for the system of property rights I have just described to be responsive to the basic personal reasons that everyone has in regard to housing, the housing market must not make the poorest members of the society unable to afford housing at all. So some provision of public housing, or some more general guarantee of minimum basic income, may be required as a condition for the system as a whole to be justifiable.

Profits from investing in housing may generate significant inequality. If this inequality has negative consequences of the kinds I have discussed in other chapters, then taxing income from the sale of property might be the best way of controlling these negative externalities. As long as this is done within the limits described, it would have the advantage of not interfering with the important reasons individuals have to want to choose and control their own housing, or with the efficiency of assigning housing to those who are most willing to pay for it. My purpose here is not to describe or assess all these reasons. The point is rather that the reasons supporting property rights in housing provide no objection in principle to taxes on profits from exchange.

I turn now to the question of taxes on income from one's job. Here we can begin with the importance of "free choice of occupation." Everyone has a strong reason to be able to choose how to spend his or her productive energies. This provides strong reason to reject laws or policies that allow people to be forced to work at a particular job, and everyone should be free to quit if he or she chooses. But what do 'forced' and 'free' mean here? It would be unacceptable to legally require individuals to work at certain jobs (except, perhaps, for emergency cases like military draft). But individuals also have reason to want to be placed in good conditions for choosing their careers. That is, they have good reasons, of the kinds I discussed in Chapter 5, to want to be informed about various kinds of work they might do, and to be able to acquire the qualifications for work that they are suited for.

On the other hand, just as with housing, people can't always have exactly the jobs they want. A market in employment allows people to choose jobs against a background of wages that reflect the costs to others of their choices. No one has to work for less than his or her reserve wage (given the alternatives) and employers do not have to pay more than a worker is worth to them. In such a system, workers with particular skills are allocated efficiently (i.e. in a way that is responsive to demand for these skills). This system allows for flexibility: labor will be shifted to different uses as the market requires, as demand and technology change.

These considerations—the reasons individuals have to want to be able to choose their own professions, and the efficiency advantages of a market in labor—do not count against taxing a portion of earnings, within certain limits. In addition to those I have mentioned, free choice of occupation requires that individuals should be able to earn more by working more or taking a second job if they prefer.[18] To prevent this, by taxing away all the extra income they could earn above a certain amount, would not be justifiable, given the reasons that individuals have to be able to act on their different preferences between work, leisure, and other forms of consumption.

It might be argued, however, that an entity with the power to tax a part of what others are willing to pay a person for his labor would be a partial owner of that person's labor, and that this would be akin to slavery, because it is incompatible with the idea of self-ownership—that individuals are the sole owners of their energies and talents and have sole discretion about how these are to be used.[19] To assess this argument we need to ask what makes the idea of self-ownership appealing, and whether the reasons that lie behind its appeal support the idea that individuals are entitled to the full amount of what others are willing to pay for their services. This is just to apply to self-ownership the same method I have been applying to the idea of equality throughout this book, and in this chapter to ideas of liberty and coercion, namely to try to identify the reasons that give these concepts their importance and to ask when these reasons apply.

It is quite plausible to say that we are owners of parts of our body, such as our eyes and our kidneys. It would be wrong for someone to take these from us without our consent, but we also have the power to give them to others, or sell them if we wish to do so. The question is in what sense we

---

[18] As argued by Anthony Atkinson in *Inequality: What Can Be Done?*, 186, 210.

[19] The claim about slavery was famously made by Nozick in *Anarchy, State, and Utopia*, 169–72. G. A. Cohen develops the idea of self-ownership as the best interpretation of Nozick's position, and argues that it does rule out taxation of earnings, although he then goes on to reject the thesis that we are self-owners in this sense. See *Self-Ownership, Freedom, and Equality*, chapters 9 and 10.

are owners of our labor, and what this implies about the justifiability of taxation.

I believe that what is plausible in the idea of self-ownership in one's labor is fully captured by considerations I have mentioned: the reasons people have to be able to choose their occupation, to be able to quit a job if they wish, and so on. These reasons explain why institutions such as slavery that deny free choice of occupation are illegitimate. But it does not follow from these considerations that workers are entitled to the "full value" of what they do—to the top wage that employers would be willing to pay, as determined by the demand for their services and the scarcity of the skills they have to offer. Taxing a portion of people's earnings is not ruled out by these reasons, and so can be legitimate if there is good reason for it.[20]

Central among these reasons, as I have said, is the need to provide the conditions required in order for the system of property and market exchange through which one's income is earned to be legitimate. I have mentioned a number of such reasons, including those provided by the negative consequences of high levels of inequality. Taxing a person for these reasons is not correctly described as forcing him to use resources that are legitimately his to help others. Rather, these taxes reflect the limits on the claims to resources that he can come to have within a legitimate system of property and market exchange.

Two particular reasons for taxation are relevant to the present discussion of self-ownership. The efficiency of a market economy requires that employers have the power to direct what their workers do, and the power to hire or fire workers in response to changes in technology and market conditions. These powers diminish individuals' ability to determine how their talents and energies are used. This affects all workers to some extent, but is particularly severe for those who have the lowest level of

---

[20] Here I am in at least partial agreement with what David Gauthier says in *Morals by Agreement*, 272–6. G. A. Cohen argues, against Gauthier, that self-ownership is incompatible with taxes on income because "persons are exclusive owners of what they own only if they are entitled to set the terms on which they will exchange what they own with one another" (*Self-Ownership, Freedom, and Equality*, 221). If "set the terms" not only means "receive what one reasonably expects to receive in making the transaction" but also "receive everything that others are willing to pay," then this does rule out taxation. But this is not supported by the reasons I have mentioned that form the basis of the appeal of "self-ownership" and explain why slavery is wrong.

marketable skills, who must take often quite disagreeable work, under the control of others, in order to obtain the means of living.

These powers are therefore things that workers have reasons—the basic reasons lying behind the idea of self-ownership—to object to. Even if these are not sufficient reason to reject such powers altogether, given the arguments in their favor, they amount to good reason to define these powers in ways that limit their effects on individuals' control over their own lives. This can, to some extent, be done by providing good public education, enabling individuals to develop a wider range of skills, hence a wider range of possible forms of employment. It could also be done by measures that increase the bargaining power of workers, such as laws that increase the power of unions, or by providing a minimum basic income to all, thereby putting even the least qualified workers in a stronger position to decline particular forms of work if they wish to do so.[21] These strategies have the advantage of letting workers themselves decide whether they want to press for higher pay or for improvements in their working conditions.

Taxes on income that are needed to provide these benefits will prevent individuals from receiving the full amount that others are willing to pay them for what they do. But, looking at the matter purely from the point of view of the reasons supporting the idea of self-ownership—in particular, reasons to want to be free from control by others—what these individuals give up is vastly less important than the gain to those who receive the benefits that these taxes make possible.

Understanding self-ownership as a "side-constraint" that must not be violated would block comparisons of this kind. But in order to decide whether we should accept such a constraint, we need to look, as I have been doing, at the reasons lying behind it. When we do this, we can see that there is not sufficient reason to accept a constraint in this general form.

[21] As argued by Philippe van Parijs in *Real Freedom for All.*

8

Desert

Inequality is sometimes justified by saying that those who have more deserve these greater benefits. N. Gregory Mankiw, for example, has recently defended high levels of compensation for CEOs on the grounds that they deserve these rewards because of their productivity.[1] On the other hand, the idea of desert might be appealed to in defense of the opposite conclusion. It might be claimed, for example, that, even if high levels of executive pay provide incentives that increase productivity, these rewards are still unjust, because no one deserves to be paid that much for doing those jobs. These two arguments draw different conclusions about just compensation, but they share the assumption that levels of economic reward are properly justified at least in part, on the basis of desert.

I will argue in this chapter that this assumption should be rejected. The word 'desert' is used to make many different kinds of claims. When these different claims are distinguished and examined carefully it will emerge that when it is true to say that a person deserves (or does not deserve) a certain economic reward, this is so because of some more general idea of justice, not itself dependent on an idea of desert. The idea of desert plays no independent role in these cases either as a justification for greater economic rewards or as a limit on them. To argue convincingly for this negative conclusion I will need first to examine the different kinds of desert claims. I can then use this understanding to explain why desert might seem to be relevant to questions of distributive justice and why this apparent relevance is mistaken.

'Desert' is sometimes used in a perfectly general sense in which to say that a person deserves a certain treatment is simply to say that he or she

[1] Mankiw, "Defending the One Percent"; Piketty, *Capital in the Twenty-First Century*, 331–5.

ought to be treated in this way, or that treating the person in this way would be just. It is true (trivially) that people ought to be treated in ways that they deserve in this general sense. But, understood in this way, claims about what people deserve leave entirely open why it is just for people to be treated in the way in question. For all that is said, the explanation might be based on utilitarianism, on Rawls's theory of justice, on a libertarian view, or on any other view about what justice requires. Claims about desert, in this general sense, are just claims about what is required by justice in some sense or other. In order to provide a distinctive basis for arguing either for or against inequality, claims about desert need to have some more specific moral content.

Another sense in which a person may be said to deserve a certain treatment is that that treatment is prescribed by some institution. For example, if the established grading policy in a class calls for any student who has an average test score higher than 95 percent to be given a grade of A, then a student whose average score is 97 percent may be said to deserve an A. Claims of this kind are what Joel Feinberg and John Rawls call claims of institutional entitlement.[2]

But not just any institution can give rise to morally valid claims of institutional entitlement. The rules of a school might dictate that the student with the lowest grade average in one semester must serve for a semester as the personal servant of the student who achieved the highest grade average. But the student who achieved the highest average would not be entitled to this service, since the institution requiring some students to be the servants of others cannot be justified. So, although claims of institutional entitlement can be true, their truth depends on the justification for the institution in question, which need not depend on an independent idea of desert. Perhaps there is a sense of desert in which institutions can be justified by the fact that they give people what they, independently, deserve in this sense. I will consider in what follows whether there might be such a sense. My present point is just that this non-institutional sense of desert would have to be different from the idea of institutional entitlement.

Another morally powerful idea closely related to the idea of institutional entitlement is the wrongfulness of failing to fulfill legitimate

---

[2] See Feinberg, "Justice and Personal Desert," 81, 85–8; and Rawls, *A Theory of Justice*, section 48, citing Feinberg.

expectations. If a student has worked hard to have an average test score above 95 percent in hopes of getting a grade of A, but then does not receive an A despite having a 96 percent average, he or she has a legitimate complaint. The force of this complaint seems to go beyond the idea of institutional entitlement, by appealing to the fact that the student has made sacrifices in expectation of this reward. (Institutional entitlement is thus a broader concept than legitimate expectation, since claims of institutional entitlement do not depend on a person's having relied in any way on that institution.) But the force of a demand based on the idea of legitimate expectation depends again on the justifiability of the institution in question. If a student had worked hard to achieve the highest average in the class, in the expectation of earning the right to have the lowest ranking student as his personal servant for the coming term, he would not have a valid complaint of the kind I am describing if he did not receive this service. He might have a legitimate objection to having been deceived about the prospect of this reward, but he would not be entitled to it, because the rule providing for it is unjustifiable.

In order to serve as a distinctive basis for assessing institutions, desert claims need to be distinct from claims of institutional entitlement or legitimate expectations. They need to be *non-institutional*, that is to say, not dependent on institutions that are justified in some other way.

Justifications based on desert, insofar as they are to be distinctive, also need to be distinguished from justifications based on the good effects of treating a person in a certain way. To discipline a child by depriving him of a treat "because he deserves it" is a different thing from doing this because it is thought that this will improve his character or make him (or his siblings) likely to behave better in future. (Thus Mankiw, in the article mentioned, distinguishes desert-based justifications for executive pay from utilitarian justifications, based on the good effects the incentives that these rewards provide.) Claims based on desert also differ in this way from claims based on need. It may be said, for example, that a person deserves help because he is starving, or that he deserves medical care because he is sick. But these justifications really appeal to the benefits of providing people with these forms of treatment. By contrast, the claim that executives deserve higher pay because of what they have done does not depend on the idea that they will benefit more from the additional money than others would.

Desert claims of the kind we are looking for, then, are claims about how people should be treated that are non-institutional (not dependent on the fact that some institution prescribes this form of treatment) and not based on the supposed benefits, to the person or others, that flow from treating such people in that way. These are what I will call *pure desert claims*—claims that a certain form of treatment is made appropriate *simply* by facts about what a person is like or has done, where the qualification 'simply' rules out justifications of the two kinds just mentioned—justifications appealing to institutions or to the good effects of treating people in the way in question. This narrowing of focus is not ad hoc, but merely reflects what appeals to desert need to be like if they are to be a distinctive form of argument for or against unequal treatment.

I believe that pure desert claims of this kind are sometimes valid. The clearest examples are desert claims regarding expressions of praise, admiration, gratitude, blame, or condemnation. If a person has acted in a certain way simply out of a desire to benefit me, and at some cost to herself, this fact by itself makes an attitude of gratitude on my part appropriate. My expression of this gratitude may please my benefactor, and may encourage her and others to act this way in the future. But these effects are not what makes my gratitude appropriate. Gratitude is called for simply by what the person did, and the attitudes that her doing this reflected. Similarly, if a person has made an important discovery or achieved some other form of excellence, this makes approval and admiration, and also expressions of these attitudes, appropriate. And the fact that a person has caused harm by acting with complete indifference to the welfare of others, or with the intention of injuring them, can make appropriate attitudes of condemnation and the suspension of friendly feelings.[3]

These judgments of appropriateness rest on the internal connection between facts about the person and the content of the reactions in question. For example, the fact that someone has gone out of her way to benefit me is connected in this way with my having feelings of gratitude toward her, and an increased willingness to benefit her should the occasion arise. And there is also such a connection between the fact

---

[3] I defend these claims at greater length in *Moral Dimensions*, chapter 4, in "Giving Desert its Due," and most recently in "Forms and Conditions of Responsibility."

that someone has repeatedly betrayed my trust and my having feelings of resentment and a decreased willingness to trust him in future.

My adoption of these negative reactive attitudes involves a cost for the people toward whom they are directed. They have reason to care about how I regard them, and changes in my attitudes, such as my diminished willingness to trust them, can also deprive them of opportunities that they have reason to want. But a person toward whom these revised attitudes are appropriate cannot reasonably object to these costs. No one has an unconditional claim to our good opinion, and trust is owed only to those who are themselves trustworthy. So someone who has betrayed another person has no moral complaint about suffering such losses.

Nor are these changes in attitude appropriate only if the features of a person to which they are responses were under the person's control.[4] They are made appropriate *simply* by facts about what that person is like or has done. I am not required to trust someone who has betrayed my trust whether or not he or she could have chosen not to be an untrustworthy person.

Facts about voluntariness and control can be relevant to the question of what attitudes, if any, a given action reflects. The fact that when he was being tortured my friend revealed things that I told him in confidence says something different about his loyalty than if he had revealed these secrets quite willingly in casual conversation, just to be amusing. And the fact that he would reveal these things when his brain was stimulated in a certain way may say nothing at all about his loyalty or his other attitudes toward me. But it is these attitudes toward me themselves that make responses of the kind I am discussing appropriate or inappropriate. In order to have this significance these attitudes need not themselves be under the person's control, nor need these features of his personality be things that he deserves to have. A desert basis need not itself be deserved.

These connections between features of what a person is like and the content of the attitudes toward him or her that these features make appropriate are matters of normative fact, not social convention. Social convention can enter, however, in determining what action will be seen as expressing a given response in a given social setting. It is a matter of

---

[4] For fuller discussion of these claims about responsibility, see the works cited in n. 3, esp. "Forms and Conditions of Responsibility."

convention that, in English, saying "Thank you" is a way of expressing gratitude. And social conventions may determine whether a gift of money to someone who has benefitted you is an expression of gratitude or an insult. But it is important to distinguish the role of normative facts and the role of social conventions in making particular responses appropriate.

If what a person has done makes the expression of a certain attitude (such as gratitude, admiration, disapproval, or condemnation) appropriate, and if acting toward the person in a certain way is, in our society, conventionally recognized as a way of expressing this attitude, then it may seem—indeed probably *will* seem to people who share this convention—that acting in this way toward the person is made appropriate by what he or she has done. This form of treatment will seem to be *deserved* in the sense I am now discussing.

That this conclusion about desert will seem to follow, to people who share the convention in question, is an important descriptive fact that we need to take account of in order to understand how things work in a given society. As I remarked in Chapter 3, if executives of large companies in a certain industry generally receive seven-figure bonuses, then it may seem to people that this is what they deserve. But it is important also to see that as a normative matter this line of thinking can involve a non-sequitur. An internal normative connection of the kind I am discussing extends only to the *content* expressed by a reaction—it renders that content not inappropriate. But from the fact that such a connection holds it does not follow that just any action that, as a matter of convention, has the relevant expressive content is therefore justified. To take a dramatic example, it may be true that stealing from one's neighbors is appropriately condemned. And in a certain society it may be held that cutting off a person's hand expresses the relevant kind of condemnation and is therefore deserved—that anything less would fail to respond to the seriousness of the crime. But this is a mistake. From the fact that cutting of a person's hand conventionally expresses a degree of condemnation that is appropriate to theft it does not follow that a practice of cutting off the hands of convicted thieves is justified.[5]

---

[5] In my view, it is a serious problem in the contemporary U.S. that conventional ideas both about the level of economic reward appropriate for certain economic roles and about the prison sentences that are appropriate condemnation for various crimes have undergone a morally disastrous level of inflation.

This claim about the limited role of desert is even more plausible in the case of "positive" responses, such as praise and admiration. The fact that a person has made an important scientific discovery makes reactions of praise and admiration appropriate. But this claim of appropriateness implies nothing about whether any particular monetary reward, or even a monetary reward of any kind, is the kind of response that is called for.

In my view, desert thus plays only a very limited role in the justification of criminal punishment. Insofar as criminal punishment involves a kind of condemnation, punishment is appropriate only for actions that merit condemnation of this kind. In this sense, punishment must be deserved. But the idea of desert plays no role either in justifying or in limiting the kind of hard treatment, such as imprisonment, that a just institution can impose for certain crimes. Imposing hard treatment as a penalty for certain crimes can be justified only by the social benefits of such a policy, and such hard treatment is limited by the cost that it is fair to impose on an individual in order to promote these benefits. It is also limited by the requirement that it can be imposed only on individuals who have been given a fair opportunity to avoid punishment. The latter requirement is not based on desert. The idea is not that people deserve punishment (in some non-institutional sense of desert) only if they have chosen to do wrong. Rather, opportunity to avoid is a condition that plays a role in the justification of any social policy. If a policy imposes burdens on some people in order to provide some general social benefit, then, wherever possible, individuals must be given adequate opportunity to avoid bearing these burdens by choosing appropriately.[6]

This view is of course controversial. Even if criminal penalties are not made appropriate simply by the fact that they express an appropriate from of condemnation, there might be some other way in which they can be justified (and limited) on grounds of desert—that is to say, some other way in which certain punishments are justified simply by facts about what a person is like, or has done. I do not believe that this is the case, but I have not argued against any particular desert claims of this kind. My purpose in this discussion has simply been to call attention to one class of pure desert claims that can be valid—namely claims about the

---

[6] For elaboration and defense of this "value of choice" account, see chapter 6 of *What we Owe to Each Other* and "Forms and Conditions of Responsibility."

appropriateness or inappropriateness of certain attitudes—and to indicate the limits of what such claims can justify.

These conclusions carry over to the case of distributive justice. The fact that a person has played a particular role in a productive economic process may be grounds for admiration or gratitude. But this does not, in itself, make any particular level of monetary reward appropriate. As I have said, certain rewards may *seem* to some people to be appropriate if, as a matter of custom, those who play that role have generally received reward of this kind. But these convention-based reactions have no justifying force. Desert claims of the particular expressive kind I have been discussing play no role in the justification of distributive shares.

As I just mentioned in the case of criminal punishment, however, even if desert arguments of this expressive kind do not justify special economic rewards, there remains the question of whether there are valid pure desert claims of some more specific kind concerning the economic rewards that individuals should receive. To answer this question I need to consider what these claims might be and, drawing on the distinctions that have been introduced so far, assess the case that might be made for them.

One desert-based argument for unequal shares that is commonly heard is that people deserve to be paid more if they have exerted greater effort than others. Anthony Atkinson, for example, writes, "Fairness involves a perceptible link between effort and reward: people deserve to keep at least a reasonable portion of what they earn through increased hours or increased responsibility or a second job."[7]

Why might this seem to be so? One answer would be that a willingness to work hard shows a kind of moral merit that deserves to be rewarded. The moral merit of an action depends on the agent's motivation for performing it, so this rationale would seem to call for higher pay for people who work hard for altruistic reasons rather than for those who do so in hopes of financial gain. It would therefore not necessarily have implications of the kind that Mankiw, for example, seemed to have in mind.

The dependence of moral merit on motive also raises the difficulty that individuals' motives are difficult to discern. Rawls cites this as a reason

---

[7] Atkinson, *Inequality: What Can Be Done?*, 186.

why a principle calling for reward in accord with merit would be "unworkable," and Hayek makes a similar point.[8] Another problem, which follows from our earlier discussion, is that the idea of moral merit provides no determinate standard for determining monetary rewards. Moral merit may deserve praise and admiration. But it does not follow that any particular amount of extra pay, or indeed any amount at all, is called for.

In addition, it might be said, perhaps for some of these same reasons, that rewarding moral virtue should not be the function of economic institutions.[9] The idea of "the function" of economic institutions may be vague. But one reason (in addition to those just mentioned) for thinking that distribution according to moral merit is not an appropriate standard of distributive justice is that a standard of just distribution must provide a reason for some to have more that others should accept as a reason for them to have less. Moral merit does not seem to provide such a justification. It may well be that moral merit, in itself, makes it appropriate for those who have it to get more praise and admiration than others do. But it does not seem to be a reason for the less meritorious to accept lower incomes.[10]

Such a reason might seem to be provided by an idea that may resemble a claim of desert but is in fact quite different. This is the idea that, if those who have lower incomes could have had the higher incomes that others enjoy if they had exerted themselves, then they cannot object to their lower earnings, since it is their fault that they have not earned more. Although this justification might sound as if it were based on the idea that greater effort deserves greater reward, it is not, or at least need not be. The idea at work is not desert but the quite different idea that might

---

[8] Rawls, *A Theory of Justice*, 274. Hayek, *The Constitution of Liberty*, 93–4.

[9] I am not denying that, as David Miller rightly points out, there is a sense of desert that is independent of institutional entitlement (*Principles of Social Justice*, chapter 7, 142–3). Thus we might say, for example, that a certain runner deserved to win the race, because she was in fact the better runner, although she did not win, and is therefore not entitled to the prize, because she was knocked off balance by a gust of wind just before the finish. And we might say, as well, that races should be organized so that the better runner is likely to win. But this is because the purpose of races is to serve as contests of athletic ability. My point is that there is no non-institutional sense of desert of this kind that should serve as a basis for determining levels of economic reward. As Miller notes (139–40), this is a point about the nature and justification of economic institutions; not something that follows from the concept of desert.

[10] A point made by Samuel Scheffler in "Justice and Desert in Liberal Theory," 191.

be called *adequate opportunity to choose*. A policy of paying people more if they work harder may be justified not on grounds of desert but because the incentives this creates improve overall productivity, or because it satisfies Rawls's Difference Principle by making the worse off better off. If this is so, then those who have less because they do not respond to these incentives by working harder may have no complaint about having less than others do, provided that just background institutions are in place. That is to say, provided that the conditions under which they choose not to exert this extra effort are not unjust.

This is a point made by Rawls in a much disputed passage that I discussed in Chapter 5, in relation to equality of opportunity, but which I will describe again here since the point is relevant and important. In the passage in question Rawls writes, "Even the willingness to make an effort, to try, and so to be deserving in the ordinary sense is itself dependent upon happy family and social circumstances."[11] A natural interpretation of this passage takes it to involve two claims: (1) that willingness to make an effort is a positive desert basis that justifies greater rewards *if* a person can claim credit for this willingness, but (2) that a person cannot claim credit for his or her willingness to make an effort if this is due to "factors outside of him or her" such as "happy family and social circumstances."

There are two problems with this. First, it is difficult to defend claim (1) as an interpretation of Rawls, given that he elsewhere argues against moral desert as a basis for distributive shares.[12] Second, claim (2) depends on the idea, which I have argued is mistaken, that a desert basis must itself be deserved.

As I argued in Chapter 5, a better interpretation is available. Individuals cannot complain about not having some benefit if this benefit has been offered to them on reasonable terms and if their decision not to accept these terms was made under sufficiently good conditions. An important role for principles of justice is to specify what is required in order for the conditions that social institutions supply to be "sufficiently good"—that is to say, in order for them to be such that the choices that individuals make under these conditions are morally binding. On this interpretation, the point Rawls is making in the passage in question is not

---

[11] *A Theory of Justice*, 74 (2nd edn, 64).
[12] See *A Theory of Justice*, section 48.

that willingness to exert oneself does not deserve reward when it is the result of (favorable) "external" causes, but rather that a *lack* of willingness to make the effort required to gain a benefit does not render it just that the person lacks that benefit unless the conditions under which the person failed to make this effort meet the requirements of justice. If some people whose circumstances are "happy" make the effort required to achieve certain benefits while others, whose circumstances are not merely less happy but unjust, do not do this, then this difference in effort does not render the resulting inequality just. This illustrates the difference between a desert-based justification for inequality and a justification based on what I am calling the idea of adequate opportunity to choose, which presupposes a standard of just conditions.

Another possible explanation for why those who exert greater effort deserve greater reward is that effort involves a sacrifice, for which people should be compensated. Requiring greater effort is not the only way in which a job can involve greater than usual sacrifices. Some kinds of work are more unpleasant than others, more dangerous, or have bad effects on a worker's health. So people in demanding white-collar jobs would not be the only, or even the main, beneficiaries of this rationale for greater reward.

In the context of our present discussion, however, there are two problems with this idea (which are not necessarily *objections* to it). The first is that on this account claims to compensation are not based on an idea of desert but rather, like claims of need discussed earlier, based on an idea of benefit (or loss). The second problem is that the idea of compensation for sacrifice is not an independent standard of justice (desert-based or not) but rather a partial principle that presupposes some other, more basic standard. This might be the idea that people are owed compensation when they have been harmed. But I will assume in the present context the relevant standard is some idea of just distribution.

So understood, the idea behind claims to compensation is that sacrifices such as those involved in exerting special effort involve losses in well-being that need to be taken into account in assessing how well off people are for purposes of applying the relevant standard of distributive justice. Suppose that this standard of justice requires outcomes in which individuals' levels of well-being fit a certain pattern (which might be equality, or some non-egalitarian pattern). The claim is that an outcome that fits this pattern only when measured without taking into account the cost of effort (or some other kind of sacrifice) is not in fact just, according to the standard in question. To achieve justice, those who have made these sacrifices should receive *more* in other terms (greater income, for example) to compensate for these sacrifices and thus bring them to the level that justice requires. If the relevant standard of justice requires equal levels of well-being, then the claim is that unequal incomes may be required in order to achieve overall equality of the kind that justice requires.

Another explanation for the significance of effort is that it represents a sacrifice that people have made in legitimate expectation of some reward, a legitimate expectation that should not be disappointed. The point is not that sacrifice calls for compensation, but that just institutions must fulfill the expectations that they invite people to act on. As I pointed out earlier, however, claims of legitimate expectation presuppose some standard of institutional legitimacy. So claims of effort understood in this way are not an independent basis for assessing institutions.

Another idea of desert is that, as Mankiw puts it, "people should receive compensation congruent with their contributions."[13] This idea has greatest plausibility when the "contributions" of different participants can be clearly distinguished. Suppose that two people cooperate to produce a product, one of them producing the inner workings, the other adding a distinctively designed outer casing. If the functionality produced by the inner workings is basically the same as other products on the market, but the distinctive design causes their product to outsell these competitors and make a great deal of money, then it seems reasonable to say that the person responsible for this design has made a greater contribution to the success of the product, and should therefore get a larger share of the profits.

But in more complex forms of cooperative production the contributions of different participants are not easily distinguishable.[14] Mankiw seems to take the contribution that a given participant's compensation should be "congruent with" to be that participant's "marginal product."

[13] "Defending the One Percent," 32.

[14] As Piketty argues. *Capital in the Twenty-First Century*, 331: "In fact it [individual marginal productivity] becomes something close to a pure ideological construct on the basis of which a justification for higher status can be elaborated."

This is the difference that adding or subtracting a unit of what that participant does would make to the value of what is produced. But as many have pointed out, this purely subjunctive idea need not correspond with what a given participant "has contributed" in the sense that seemed to apply in my first example.[15]

Suppose that a productive process involves a number of workers who, while they are working, cannot always see what others are doing. It may be that these workers would work more efficiently (would accomplish more with a given amount of total labor) if someone helped to coordinate their efforts by standing at a place where she can see and be seen by all of the workers, and signaling to them what most needs to be done at a given time. The marginal product of this coordinator would be the value of the increased production resulting from a unit of time of her "direction." That is to say, the difference in value between what the workers would produce in that time if they are directed and what they would produce in that time without direction. Perhaps the marginal product of the person in this directing role is greater than that of the ordinary workers. But the extra quantity of goods produced as a result of this direction is not something "produced by" the person who provides the direction. Rather, it is produced by the other workers with her help. What the marginal productivity of a worker in this sense does identify is the maximum it would be rational for a profit-maximizing firm to pay, at the margin, for the services of such a worker. But it does not follow that if the worker does not receive this he or she is being cheated, or "deprived of the fruits of his or her labor."[16]

I have assumed in this example that the job done by the person who provides direction requires no special skill. She is just standing in a

[15] See, among others, Nozick, *Anarchy, State, and Utopia*, 187n., and Amartya Sen, "The Moral Standing of the Market," 15–17, and "Just Deserts." I take Nozick's view, as indicated in the last sentence of the footnote just cited, to be that if, in a competitive economy, individuals receive rewards proportional to their marginal product, this outcome will be just *because* it results from a process of free exchange in accord with an entitlement conception of justice, not because of the relation of these rewards to marginal products.

[16] As Sen points out in "Just Deserts," this is even clearer when what one person "contributes" is just permission to use something that he or she owns. If, for example, a person owns a strip of land between a field and a factory where work is done, much time may be saved if workers can cross his land rather than go around it. What he "contributes" in what Nozick calls the "subjunctive" sense (the difference made by his giving permission to cross his land) may be quite large even though he does not "produce" anything.

different place from the other workers, and is thus able to see what is needed at a given time in order to keep the production process going smoothly. It may seem that things would be different in the case of a person who played a similar role in virtue of having some special skill, such as an ability to discern quickly the best way to move the work forward. Having this skill might be something to be proud of. It would be worthwhile for a firm or perhaps a society to invest in training through which people would develop this ability, and worthwhile to choose people who have developed it for this "directing" role, a role that might be more desirable than other jobs in the production process because it is less physically demanding and because it offers "powers and prerogatives of office" that allow for the exercise of this realized capacity. Creating this position, and offering the kind of training needed to fill it, would therefore, in itself, constitute a kind of inequality. The further question is whether, in addition to this kind of inequality, the person who fills this role should be paid more than others, and in particular whether she should be paid more because her marginal product is greater than that of other workers. The answer to the latter question seems to me to be "no." The fact that a special skill is required does not change the fact that the "marginal product" of the "director" remains a purely subjunctive notion, just as in my earlier example.

This brings us to the idea that individuals can deserve greater economic rewards because they have special abilities. Why might this be so? And what abilities would these be? Some kinds of ability, in art, science, engineering, and perhaps in organization and management as well, may be excellences that deserve our praise and admiration. But, as I have argued, it does not follow from this that any particular economic reward, or any economic reward at all, is called for.

On the other hand, there may be positions for which special powers, special opportunities, or even special economic rewards may be justified by the benefits they bring—by their economic efficiency, or by the fact that they satisfy Rawls's Difference Principle or some other standard of distributive justice. If this is so, then there will be a "top-down" argument of the kind I discussed in Chapter 4 for selecting people for these positions on the basis of their ability, and those who have ability of the relevant kind can be therefore said to deserve to be chosen for these positions. "Ability" in the sense in question here will not be an intrinsically valuable characteristic of certain individuals, but rather defined in an institution-dependent way as those traits, whatever they may be, that make a person likely to perform well in the position in question. The claim to be rewarded on the basis of desert is in this case a claim of institutional entitlement rather than desert.

In this chapter, I have addressed the question of whether the idea of desert provides a distinct basis for justifying unequal rewards or placing a limit on them. In order to play this role, an idea of desert would need to be different from the perfectly general idea of what people ought (for whatever reason) to have. Distinctively desert-based justifications also need to be different from justifications that depend on what is prescribed by institutions that are justified in some other way, and from justifications based on the good consequences of treating people in certain ways. Some pure desert claims of this kind are valid, in particular, claims about the praise, gratitude, blame, or condemnation that people deserve. But I argued that neither differential economic rewards nor particular forms of criminal punishment can be justified in this way.

I then considered various specific desert-based justifications for extra reward: justifications based on moral merit, effort, ability, and contribution. In each case, my strategy has been to consider why these characteristics might seem to be a basis for special reward, and to argue that on closer examination none of them is a valid desert-based justification for special economic benefit. I am not arguing that all claims about equality that are formulated in terms of desert are false or mistaken. As I said earlier, many such claims may be quite true. What I have questioned is whether these claims are based on a distinctive moral idea of desert.

Consider, for example, Anthony Atkinson's remark, which I quoted earlier, that "people deserve to keep at least a reasonable portion of what they earn through increased hours or increased responsibility or a second job." The best interpretation of this remark is not as a claim about desert, in a non-institutional sense. A defensible economic system has to offer everyone the opportunity to earn more money if they wish to do so. This opportunity is particularly important for the poor, but it is important for everyone, rich and poor alike. It would be unfair to deny people this opportunity to increase their pretax income and doubly unfair (a violation of legitimate expectations) to tax away all of the benefits gained in this way. The latter point is brought home with particular force by Atkinson's examples of people seeking to become richer by *working* more or working harder, which might suggest that his objection to higher rates of effective taxation applies only to taxes on earned income. But the same point (about legitimate expectations) might be made with examples of people who forego consumption to make money by investing, provided that the institutions that allow for income from investments of this kind are independently justified.

9

Unequal Income

Inequality in the United States and other developed economies has increased greatly in recent decades. In 2014, 21.2 percent of total income (from wages, salaries, interest dividends and profits from sales) in the United States went to the top 1 percent of earners, and 4.9 percent went to the top 0.01 percent. This was a significant increase in inequality. According to the Congressional Budget Office, in the period 1979–2014, the before-tax incomes of the top 1 percent increased by 174.5 percent, while the before-tax incomes of those in the bottom 20 percent increased by only 39.7 percent. (Income in these cases includes government transfers, such as welfare payments.) The difference in growth of after-tax incomes was even sharper, with the incomes of the top 1 percent increasing by 200.2 percent and those of the bottom 20 percent increasing by only 48.2 percent. (The increase for those between the bottom 21 percent and the bottom 80 percent was only 40 percent.) At the end of this period, the average annual income (before taxes and transfers) of people in the top 0.1 percent was $6,087,113, twenty times the average income even of the top 10 percent as a whole.[1]

This increase in inequality represents a number of distinct phenomena. These include, first, increased compensation of top managers in large firms (what Piketty calls "supermanagers"[2]), second, the rise and increased profitability of the financial sector, and, third, an increase in the share of national income that takes the form of returns to capital.

Here are some facts about the first of these, which I mentioned in Chapter 1. The average compensation of executives in the 350 largest

[1] Figures are from the Congressional Budget Office and from Emmanuel Saez, "Striking it Richer: The Evolution of Top Incomes in the United States (Updates with 2014 Preliminary Estimates)." Accessed at Inequality.org.
[2] *Capital in the Twenty-First Century*, 298–300.

firms in the U.S. in 1965 was twenty times the average compensation of workers in those firms. This ratio "peaked at 376 to 1 in 2000." In 2014 it was 303 to 1, "higher than it had been at any time during the 1960s, 1970s, 1980s or 1990s."[3] Also, "From 1978 to 2014, inflation adjusted compensation increased 997 percent, a rise almost double stock market growth and substantially greater than the painfully slow 10.5 percent growth in a typical worker's annual compensation over the same period."[4] This degree of inequality seems clearly troubling. The question is why it should be troubling, and whether this can be explained by the objections I have discussed in previous chapters.

Consider first those objections to inequality based on its consequences. What is objectionable about the inequality just described does not seem to me to be that it gives rise to objectionable status harms. As I argued in Chapter 3, the poor in the United States today do suffer from such harms—from what Jiwei Ci called status poverty and agency poverty. But this does not seem to be due to the high incomes of the very rich, or to the difference between their incomes and those of the poor. The rich do live very differently from the rest of us, especially from the very poor, but the way they live does not set a standard relative to which we have reason to feel that our own lives are deficient. The standard relative to which the poor suffer from status poverty and agency poverty is set by the way that "most people" are able to live, not by the lifestyles of the super rich. The problem with this inequality is thus not that it gives rise to objectionable differences in status.

Extreme income inequality is a threat to equality of opportunity to qualify for positions of advantage. This was already a problem in 1970, given the level of inequality that existed at that time. As I argued in Chapter 5, responding to this would require providing high-quality public education and good conditions for early childhood development for all children, in addition to ensuring that the selection of individuals for higher education and for positions of advantage more generally is procedurally fair.

These things are difficult to achieve, and increased inequality, through its effects on the political system (which I will turn to next) may make it even less likely that they will be achieved by, for example, making it less

---

[3] Lawrence Mishel and Alyssa Davis, "Top CEOs Make 300 Times More than Typical Workers," 2.

[4] Mishel and Davis, "Top CEOs," 1–2.

likely that public schools will be properly funded. If these things *were* achieved, however, it is not clear that the increase in inequality brought about by the recent increase in incomes of those at the very top of the income distribution would threaten equality of opportunity. As I argued in Chapter 5, there is a limit to the amount of spending on education that could give children of the rich a significant advantage in a system that was otherwise fair. The recent increase in inequality may, however, threaten equality of opportunity in the broader sense that is concerned with opportunity to compete in the market by starting businesses, since it creates a class of extremely wealthy families with access to capital that others entirely lack.

Turning now to the question of political equality, the recent increase in incomes of those at the very top of the income distribution is due in part to political decisions, including laws and policies weakening the power of labor unions, decreased regulation of the financial industry, and changes in tax laws decreasing the marginal tax rate on very high incomes and decreasing the inheritance tax. These changes, beginning in the 1980s, reflected what was already a disproportionate influence of the rich on politics. Insofar as this is so, the recent rise in inequality is largely due to the effects of *preexisting* inequality of influence on political outcomes.

This increase may, however, make the situation worse. The increasing difference between what the rich can spend to influence political outcomes and what others can spend increases the likelihood that elected officials will be individuals whose outlooks reflect the interests of the rich, either because they are rich themselves or because they are selected for support by rich contributors. This is objectionable in itself, as a form of political unfairness, and also because it makes it less likely that political outcomes will fulfill other requirements of justice, such as equal concern and substantive opportunity. This seems to me to be the strongest of the objections to rising inequality that I have discussed so far.

Another strong objection is that this degree of inequality gives the rich objectionable forms of control over the lives of those who have less. In addition to political influence, just discussed, this also includes control over the economic system. This is particularly true of the third kind of inequality, which Piketty emphasizes, the concentration of capital in the hands of a small number of extremely rich families.

These objections to inequality based on its consequences fail to account for the sense many have that the recent rise in inequality is objectionable in itself, apart from whatever effects it may have. To assess this objection we need to turn to the idea that unequal incomes can be objectionable simply on the ground that they are unfair, and to the question of how this idea of fairness should be understood.

If partners in a business enterprise have made the same investment of money and time, then it is plausible to say that a fair mechanism for dividing the profits should give each partner an equal share. One might say that a society as a whole is like this—that it is a cooperative enterprise for mutual benefit, and that members of a society, as participants in this enterprise, should be rewarded in proportion to what they contribute. But the rationale for equal shares in this imagined case of a firm does not carry over to the case of a society as a whole, for at least two reasons.

First, I imagined that the members of the firm made the same investment of money and time, and, one might add, of talent. It can be objected that these assumptions do not hold in the case of society as a whole, since participants in social cooperation make very different contributions of resources and abilities. But second, and more fundamentally, the analogy with the firm is inappropriate because social cooperation is not an enterprise that individuals join, contributing their predefined resources and talents. Which resources individuals own, what counts as an economically valuable talent, and what abilities individuals see themselves as having reason to develop, are all determined by the institutions of a society—by laws determining property rights, forms of economic organization such as limited liability corporations, and by the particular institutions that arise within this framework. These are parts of what Rawls calls the basic structure of a society. The question we are addressing is what such a structure needs to be like in order to be fair. So the relevant idea of fairness cannot be specified in terms of ideas of ownership that depend on some particular structure of this kind.

The claims of members of society as participants in a cooperative scheme can have a role in answering this question, however. Their interests, in particular their interest in having a greater share in the fruits of social cooperation, need to be taken into account, and given equal standing, in determining what the norms of social cooperation should be. This is not to assume, at the outset, that they must have equal shares, but only that their interests must be taken into account in a fair way in answering the question of what the process that determines these shares should be like.

Rawls's argument for his Difference Principle in *A Theory of Justice* expressed one form of this idea. Rawls argued that principles of distribution would be fair if they were ones that the cooperating members of a society would choose without knowing their places in society.[5] He gave this idea more specific form in his idea of the Original Position in which principles of justice are chosen.[6]

The parties in the Original Position, as Rawls defines it, are citizens or representatives of citizens in particular social positions. In choosing principles of justice, they are motivated only by the aim of doing as well as possible for themselves or those they represent. But the Veil of Ignorance deprives them of knowledge of the particular talents or the position in society of those they represent. This motivational assumption reflects the idea that their interests in having greater shares are taken into account in the choice of principles, and the Veil of Ignorance reflects the idea that these interests have equal standing in determining what those principles should be.

Rawls argued that, under these conditions, the parties in the Original Position would have no reason to accept a principle according to which some would have less than they would have received under an equal distribution. So a principle requiring equal rewards of all social positions would be a natural first solution. But the parties would have reason to move away from this "benchmark of equality," since no one could object to inequalities that did not make them worse off (assuming that other factors, such as basic liberties, were not affected). Rawls therefore concludes that the parties in the Original Position would choose his Difference Principle as the standard of distributive justice. This principle holds that a basic structure S is just only if the inequalities that it involves are to the advantage of those in the worst off social position—that is to say, only if those who would be worst off under any alternative to S that reduced these inequalities would be worse off than those in the worst off social position under S.[7]

---

[5] *A Theory of Justice*, section 4, 2nd edn, 15–16.

[6] Spelled out in *A Theory of Justice*, in chapter 3.

[7] *A Theory of* Justice, 2nd edn, 72. Rawls also requires that positions to which special benefits are attached should be "open to all under conditions of fair equality of opportunity," a requirement that I discuss at length in Chapters 4 and 5.

Assuming, as seems very plausible, that the incomes of CEOs in our current system could be reduced in a way that would increase, or at least not reduce, the incomes of workers, this principle would explain why the inequality I have described is unjust. This account leaves us with a puzzle, however. Many people find the degree of inequality that I have described objectionable even though they do not accept anything as demanding as Rawls's Difference Principle, or his argument for it. One explanation might be that these people are unsure about exactly what fairness requires, but they think that, *whatever* the right account of fairness may be, these particular outcomes could not be called fair.[8] This raises the question of whether what is objectionably unfair about this inequality can be explained in some other way, and the question of what relation this explanation would bear to the one Rawls gives.

On my relational view of inequality, as on Rawls's view, the objection is not to the bare fact of inequality but to the institutions that produce it.[9] It does not seem to me plausible that there is a particular pattern that the distribution of income produced by a complex economy must take in order to be just. And even in the case of a single firm, it does not seem to me, in general, that there is a particular answer to what ratio there should be between the incomes of managers, workers, and shareholders. Rather, inequality is objectionable, and unfair, when the institutional mechanisms generating it cannot be justified in the right way.[10]

---

[8] I am indebted to Joshua Cohen for very helpful conversations about this question.

[9] Rawls writes, "The difference principle specifies no definite limits within which the ratio of the shares of the more and less advantaged is to fall" (*Justice as Fairness: A Restatement*, 68). Piketty also writes, "I want to insist on this point: the key issue is the justification of inequalities rather than their magnitude as such" (*Capital in the Twenty-First Century*, 264).

[10] Here, as I said in Chapter 1, I disagree with G. A. Cohen's view that inequalities that do not result from the choices of those who have less are unjust in themselves, independent of the character of the institutions that generate them. On the view I have stated, the justice or injustice of inequalities in income can depend on facts about the consequences of the institutional policy that produces it, and the consequences of alternative policies. This is not, I think, inconsistent with Cohen's view about the fact-insensitive character of (fundamental) principles of justice. (See *Rescuing Justice and Equality*, chapter 6.) I would agree that the principle I have stated, which holds that the justice of inequalities depends on these facts about consequences, is itself fact-insensitive. (Even though, as a contractualist, I may believe that some other fundamental moral principles are fact-sensitive.) The more basic disagreement in this particular case may be over which fact-insensitive principle is correct (and thus over which kind of fact non-fundamental conclusions about justice can plausibly depend). On this see n. 20 of this chapter.

So I start from the idea that an institution is unfair if it produces significant differences in income and wealth for which no sufficient reason can be given. Such inequalities might be termed "arbitrary," meaning by this that they lack proper justification. From this starting point, we can then give content to, or at least circumscribe, a notion of fair institutions by specifying what does and what does not count as a good reason for inequality of income. (This allows for the fact that where such reasons exist the pursuit of greater *equality* would be unjustifiable.) I will first consider possible justifications for institutions that generate inequality in pretax incomes, returning later to the question of taxation.

The justification for the components of a basic structure that generates pretax incomes (what I called in Chapter 7 a system of "predistribution") must take into account the reasons that all those whose lives depend on the system[11] have to want access to a larger share of resources as well as considerations of individual liberty. These include both the reasons individuals have for wanting a wider range of options to be available to them, and reasons to object to being under the control of others. What other reasons might be included?

[11] Who are those whose reasons must be taken into account in determining whether a basic structure is justified? The answer is: all those who are governed by its requirements and whose prospects in life are determined by the conditions and opportunities that it provides. In short, it includes all those for whom, as Buchanan says, it is "the only game in town" ("Rules for a Fair Game: Contractarian Notes on Distributive Justice," 130). This includes people who receive income by occupying various positions in the economy, such as worker, manager, or shareholder. It also includes those who do unpaid work, such as caring for others, that is needed to keep the society running. Children, and adults who are disabled or beyond working age, are automatically included because they do not represent separate classes of people. Rather, childhood and old age are stages in the life of every normal person. So everyone has reasons to be cared for and receive good education as a child and to be taken care of in old age, and being disabled is something that can happen to anyone. Also included among those whose reasons are to be taken into account are people, such as the Malibu surfers whom van Parijs imagines (in "Why Surfers Should Be Fed: The Liberal Case for an Unconditional Basic Income"), who choose not to play any productive role in society. The fact that they are included in this way does not settle the question of whether they should be provided with basic income or other public benefits if they choose not to work. Responding to their reasons may require only that they have access to income by choosing to work, and that they are placed in good enough conditions to make this choice. (See the discussion of "willingness" in Chapter 5.) This last condition explains why it can be just to make willingness to work a condition for public benefits for surfers, but not for those who grow up in unjust conditions such as those of the black ghettos in the United States. (See Tommie Shelby, *Dark Ghettos*, chapter 6.)

In Chapter 4, in discussing the first level of a three-level justification for positions of unequal advantage, I allowed "for purposes of completeness" that such a justification might be based in part on ideas of property rights or desert that are independent of institutions. Arguments I have given in subsequent chapters rule out these alternatives. I argued in Chapter 8 that there is no notion of desert, independent of institutions, that can play this justificatory role, and I argued in Chapter 7 that there are no non-institutional property rights that can serve as the basis for justifying or criticizing economic institutions. The reasons that can serve as such a basis, however, include the individual interests that give rise to the idea that there are such rights, such as reasons individuals have for wanting to be assured of stability in their various personal possessions, and the institutionally defined rights that are justified by these interests.

Nozick's example of Wilt Chamberlain illustrates this point. The transactions between Wilt and his fans may lead to an increase in inequality. But, as Nozick says, there are strong reasons not to interfere with this inequality in pretax incomes insofar as it comes about simply from Wilt's exercising his right to decide whether or not to play basketball for a given price and his fans exercising their rights to spend their money on tickets to see him. (As I argued in Chapter 7, the legitimacy of taxing Wilt's income is another matter.)

This may explain why many people do not object to the large incomes of sports and entertainment figures in the way that they may object to the incomes of business executives and financiers. This is not, as Mankiw suggests,[12] because the pretax incomes of sports and entertainment figures are seen as deserved (in a sense of desert that is prior to institutions and can be used to justify the rewards that these institutions assign). Rather, these pretax incomes are seen as unobjectionable insofar as, like Wilt Chamberlain's income as Nozick imagines it, they are seen as resulting simply from transactions between willing providers of a service and willing consumers, which it would be wrong to interfere with (rather than being due to laws creating intellectual property rights and cable television monopolies).

Inequalities can also be justified by the fact that they arise from the exercise of rights and powers that are required for economic productivity.

---

[12] In "Spreading the Wealth Around: Reflections Inspired by Joe the Plumber," 295.

A basic structure does not merely allocate some independently existing set of benefits.[13] It is also a system for producing benefits by making possible and encouraging forms of interaction through which material benefits are produced. Inequalities can in principle be justified by the fact that they are produced by features that are required in order to do this.[14] But it matters who enjoys these benefits. The fact that a system of rights would promote economic development, such as increased GDP, does not count in favor of that system of rights regardless of how that increased benefit would be distributed. The fact that a certain system of productive rights would promote development would not count in its favor, for example, if the increased benefits would (avoidably) all go to the President. So it is not enough to say that those who benefit from the inequality *could* compensate the losers in a way that would leave everyone better off.[15] It is necessary at least that the features of the basic structure that generate it enable the economic system to function in a way that *actually* makes everyone better off.

These two possibilities can be put together into a *necessary* condition for features of a basic structure that generate significant inequalities: it must be true either that these inequalities could not be eliminated without infringing important personal liberties,[16] or that they are required in order for the economic system to function in a way that benefits all. Inequalities that are not supported by reasons of either of these kinds benefit people in certain economic positions in ways that others have no reason to accept. Such benefits might be said to be "arbitrary" in the sense mentioned earlier: there is no sufficient reason why these people should benefit rather than others.

---

[13] A charge made by Nozick, thinking of it, incorrectly, as a criticism of Rawls. See *Anarchy, State, and Utopia*, 149–50.

[14] A point made by Marx, when he writes (in *Critique of the Gotha Program*, 531) that "Any distribution whatever of the means of consumption is only a consequence of the distribution of the conditions of production themselves." Rawls makes a similar point when he emphasizes that what he is proposing is not a standard of "allocative justice." See *A Theory of Justice*, 56 and 77, and *Justice as Fairness: A Restatement*, 50–2.

[15] What is called Kaldor-Hicks compensation. See J. R. Hicks, The Foundations of Welfare Economics," *Economic Journal*, 49 (1939), 696–712; and Nicholas Kaldor, "Welfare Propositions of Economics and Interpersonal Comparisons of Utility," *Economics Journal*, 49 (1939), 549–52.

[16] Of the kind defended in Chapter 7.

This disjunctive condition is a relatively weak interpretation of Rawls's idea that a system that generates inequalities must be "to everyone's advantage."[17] Rawls's preferred interpretation of this idea, the Difference Principle, is stronger. It requires that a system that generates inequalities must not only benefit all, but must benefit those who have less as much as possible. The inequalities that a system generates are "excessive" if they could be reduced in a way that would benefit those who have less.[18] Even the weaker requirement I have stated, however, is quite strong. It is sufficient to explain why many people see the inequalities I described at the beginning of this chapter as objectionable, without accepting a principle as strong as the one Rawls offers. They believe that these inequalities are unfair because they arise from features of our economic system that benefit only the rich.

Whether they are correct in this belief depends on empirical facts about how the economy operates and how it would operate if certain changes were made. This is a general consequence of the conception of fairness that I have proposed. Unlike alternative conceptions that identify fairness or justice with some particular pattern of outcomes, this conception makes conclusions about fairness depend on complex empirical questions about how economic institutions do function and how they could function if arranged differently. (Rawls's Difference Principle has this same feature.) For this reason, the following discussion of the fairness of current forms of inequality will be more conjectural than the more thoroughly normative investigations in previous chapters. My aim will be to identify the empirical claims on which the justifiability of current inequalities in income depends, on the view I am offering.

The increase in inequality of income described at the beginning of this chapter involves a number of distinct phenomena: increasing disparity between the wages of workers and managers, an increase in size and profitability of the financial sector, increasing returns to capital, and the rise of inherited wealth. I will focus here, as an example, on the first of these. This disparity in incomes is due to two kinds of factors: factors determining, and holding down, the wages of workers, and factors determining

---

[17] *A Theory of Justice*, section 12. This could be seen as a higher-level version of the requirement of equal concern: "higher-level" in applying to economic systems as a whole rather than to particular governmental policies.

[18] *A Theory of Justice*, 2nd edn, 68.

the compensation of top managers, and allowing these to rise. Consider first, factors affecting the highest incomes.

The compensation of executives in the largest firms has increased greatly since the 1970s. There have been great changes in the economy since that time, including changes in technology, the growth of global markets, and increases in the size of the largest firms. It might be claimed that this increase in the size of firms has brought an increase in the marginal productivity of executives running these firms, and that this justifies the increase in their compensation. But this is not a valid justification, for two reasons. First, as Piketty observes, the individual marginal productivity of an executive in such a position is very difficult to define.[19] Second, and more fundamentally, even if we could measure the marginal productivity of executives in the purely subjunctive sense— that is to say, measure the difference that it makes whether their jobs are done well or badly—marginal productivity in this merely subjunctive sense does not in itself justify greater reward. As I argued in Chapter 8, the difference it would make if one person's work were subtracted does not identify a product produced by that person, as opposed to the others involved in the process.

I have said that features of an economic system that generate significant inequalities can be justified by the fact that they are required in order for that system to be productive in a way that benefits all. Firms need to have the power to choose their executives and to decide how much to pay them, and it might be claimed that the present levels of executive compensation arise from the legitimate exercise of these powers because these greater rewards are needed as incentives to attract talented individuals to take executive positions and perform well in them. As Bivens and Mishel point out, however, the evidence is that talented individuals would be still attracted to these positions if the norms of compensation were different and executives generally received much lower levels of compensation.[20] In addition, as they also point out,

---

[19] Piketty, *Capital in the Twenty-First Century*, 330–1.

[20] Bivens and Mishel, "The Pay of Corporate Executives and Financial Professionals as Evidence of Rents in Top 1 Percent Incomes," 63. Given the inherent desirability of these positions, individuals have good reason to seek them without the inducement of large monetary rewards. It therefore seems extremely unlikely that a policy of not providing such rewards, consistently adhered to, would fail to yield a sufficient number of qualified applicants. *Given this fact*, a policy of providing large rewards would be unjustified, on

the rise and fall of compensation for CEOs in a major corporation tracks the stock prices of firms in the general sector in which that firm operates, rather than the relative success of that particular firm within that sector. So what is being rewarded is not the quality of management decisions but the luck of being in a sector of the economy in which firms in general are doing well.

Changes in technology, the growth of global markets, and the increase in the size of firms, have affected all the industrialized societies. But the rise in compensation of top executives has been much greater in some societies than in others: greater in the English-speaking countries in general and greatest of all in the United States.[21] This makes it plausible to think, as Piketty suggests, that the recent increases in executive compensation are strongly affected by the norms governing the compensation that is appropriate for individuals in these positions that are accepted in these countries, and by changes in these norms over time. This is very plausible given the way in which the compensation of top executives is increasingly set, namely by compensation committees, often employing outside consultants, who recommend and justify compensation packages on the basis of what executives are receiving at "comparable" firms.[22]

The conclusion that inequalities arising in this way are objectionable does not rest on the supposition that executive compensation results from a kind of corrupt self-dealing. What I have said is quite compatible with its being the case that compensation committees are genuinely independent of the executives whose incomes they determine and operate according to standards that they see as objectively justified. The point is rather that the mechanism that generates their increased pay lacks appropriate justification. A mechanism for determining executive compensation that has this much "slack" in it is not necessary in order for firms to function well, nor would changing it in order to reduce inequality involve any objectionable reduction in individual liberty.

---

the account I am offering. So it would be unjust to give in to demands of the sort that G. A. Cohen describes the rich as making in "Where the Action is." I do not regard the dependence of this conclusion on the fact in question (about how talented individuals would respond to a consistent policy of not offering rewards) as troubling. But Cohen might disagree.

[21] Piketty, *Capital in the Twenty-First Century*, 315–21.

[22] As I discussed in Chapter 3. See Bivens and Mishel, "Pay of Corporate Executives," 64. On possible explanations for the rise in executive pay, see also Lucian Bebchuk and Yaniv Grinstein, "The Growth of Executive Pay."

Executive compensation in the largest U.S. firms is not unique in being open to this objection. Many other incomes (including those of university professors) may be set in ways that are responsive in large part to conventional norms rather than to what is needed for institutions to function well. What is special about the compensation of CEOs is the magnitude of the incomes involved. This suggests that the strength of this particular objection to inequality (the charge of "arbitrariness") is proportional to the magnitude of the inequality involved.

One consequence of the lack of justification for the high levels of executive compensation is to undermine objections to taxing this income, such as objections that these taxes would interfere with economic efficiency. But this leaves the question of what reason there is *for* taxing these incomes at a high rate. The first, very strong reason is that taxes are required in order to pay for public goods that are necessary in order for conditions for the economic system as a whole to be justifiable, such as conditions required by equal concern and substantive opportunity. (I will say more about these later.) The reduction in the marginal tax rates for the highest earners in the United States since the 1970s was part of a more general reduction in taxes that undermined the government's ability to fulfill these requirements. Higher taxes on those in the top income brackets alone not would not be enough to solve this problem, but they would be part of any justifiable way of doing so.

A second possible justification for high marginal rates of taxation on the highest incomes is that they are needed in order to reduce the negative consequences of inequality, such as effects on the fairness of the political system. I will not say more about this here since I have already discussed objections to inequality based on its effects.

A third possible justification would be that taxes on high incomes are needed simply to prevent inequalities that are unfair in themselves. Although justifications of this kind may sometimes be valid, it is worth pointing out that taxes that "redistribute" income, even ones that do so for egalitarian reasons, need not be justified in this more controversial way. The claim in such cases would be that certain features of a basic structure that generate these unequal pretax incomes are justifiable only if a portion is redistributed by taxation. The plausibility of this justification would depend on an explanation of why these pretax incomes are justified in the first place and cannot be limited.

The case of executive compensation that we have just been discussing might be an example. Firms need to have the authority to decide whom to hire as executives and how much they are to be paid. If there is no way to regulate this power to prevent unjustified increases, then the only way to curb the resulting inequality (assuming that there are other reasons for doing this) would be by taxing these incomes heavily. If, as has been suggested,[23] the decrease in marginal tax rates since the 1980s has been one cause of the rise in executive compensation, by giving executives greater incentives to seek higher pay and bonuses, then raising these rates would be a way of curbing this rise by decreasing these incentives.

I turn now to factors affecting the income of workers and the incomes of the poor more generally. Within the framework I am proposing, the question is whether factors that have increased inequality by holding down the incomes of workers and of those in the poorest deciles are required for economic productivity that benefits everyone, the workers and the poor included. Given the economic system we have in the contemporary United States, the share of a firm's income going to workers is determined either by bargaining between firms and individual workers, who generally have little bargaining power, or by collective bargaining between firms and unions, backed by the threat of strikes. This means that the degree of inequality that results depends heavily on the effectiveness of unions, and the failure of workers' pay to rise more than it has over the period in question has been due at least in part to laws and policies that have weakened this power.[24] Declining power of unions is only one reason why the poor in general have fared badly in recent decades, since many of the poor are unemployed. But it is one important factor.[25]

---

[23] By Piketty, *Capital in the Twenty-First* Century, 509–10, and Atkinson, *Inequality: What is to be Done?*, 186.

[24] Bruce Western and Jake Rosenfeld estimate that 1/5 to 1/3 of the increase in income inequality between 1973 and 2007 was due to declining unionization. See "Unions, Norms, and the Rise in U.S. Wage Inequality." Interestingly, they also find that increased unionization in an area is connected with higher wages for non-union workers in that area. They suggest that this is partly due to the impact of unions on labor market norms that "sustain the labor market as a social institution, in which norms of equity shape the allocation of wages outside the union sector" (p. 533). I am grateful to Charles Beitz for calling their work to my attention.

[25] Another possible factor is a reduction in the number of firms in various markets, and consequent decrease in competition for workers, which depresses workers' bargaining power, and hence their wages. See Council of Economic Advisers Policy Brief 2016,

It might be argued, in response, that greater power for unions would interfere with the efficiency of the economy by, for example, enabling workers to block changes that improve the efficiency of production. This is, as I have said, a possible justification for limiting the power of unions even if this depresses workers' income. But the experience of other countries, such as Germany, suggests that it is not in fact necessary, in order to have a well-functioning modern economy, to weaken unions in a way that drives down the income share of workers to this degree. But even if factors reducing the bargaining power of workers, and hence their incomes, are required for increased productivity, this would justify the resulting inequalities, on the view I am advocating, only if this productivity benefits all, including those whose incomes are reduced. The figures I have cited indicate that gains in productivity in recent decades have not in fact been shared by those in the lowest income groups. Real pretax income of men in the bottom 50 percent of the income distribution in the United States was no higher in 2015 than it was in 1962.[26]

It might be argued that, given international competition, higher pay for workers would not in fact make them better off. Instead, it would raise the cost of production and hence the price of the goods in question, with the result that the firms employing them would no longer be competitive and their jobs would be lost. Even if this provided a justification for lower wages for workers, it would not justify lower *incomes*. If low wages allow firms to remain profitable, these profits could be shared by the workers. This could be achieved by workers owning shares in the company, or through ownership of shares by a sovereign wealth fund, which would use the profits to pay for income supplements or other measures I have mentioned, or to provide a higher level of public services, including health care, public transportation, and free higher education that would make workers' standard of living less dependent on their income.[27]

"Labor Market Monopsony: Trends, Consequences, and Policy Responses." This would need to be addressed through anti-trust policy.

[26] See Piketty, Saez, and Zucman, "Distributional and National Accounts: Methods and Estimates for the United States."

[27] Atkinson discusses using a sovereign wealth fund in this way in *Inequality,* 176–8. He also points out (p. 161) that one cost of the former strategy (increased stock ownership by workers) is that some of the profits would be siphoned off by financial services companies who would serve as intermediaries.

This is best seen not just as question of unfair distribution of income but more generally as a matter of unfair distribution of the costs of economic productivity. In order to have an efficient economy, firms need to be able to hire and fire workers as conditions change. But there is no good reason why the cost of this flexibility should be borne only by workers. Insofar as the problem is financial—a matter of lower wages and lost income due to unemployment—it can be addressed through a system of unemployment benefits, or by a guaranteed basic income. But the costs in question are not only financial. The likelihood of being laid off when a factory closes or shifts to a different form of production deprives people of control over their lives. Effective retraining programs for workers who are laid off would alleviate this problem to some degree. But these will be helpful only if there are jobs available for workers who complete these programs. So an adequate response must also include measures, such as monetary and fiscal policy, to stimulate demand and make jobs available.

To sum up this discussion: At least three kinds of measures are required to prevent, or at least alleviate, inequality that consists of unjustifiably allowing the costs of economic productivity to fall on certain classes of workers: some form of financial cushion, such as unemployment benefits or guaranteed basic income, effective programs through which laid-off workers can acquire new skills, and more general economic policies to provide new forms of employment for those who acquire the relevant skills. The taxes required to pay for these benefits would be justified in the first of the ways I mentioned: they pay for conditions that are required in order for the economic system as a whole to be justifiable. The charge of unfairness against current policies that depress the incomes of workers depends on the claim that such measures could be implemented in a way that would leave them better off than under the current system.

There is a convergence here of reasons supporting three objections to inequality that I have distinguished. The objection I have been discussing is an objection to unjustified, hence unfair, distribution of the costs of productive efficiency. The availability of programs through which workers can acquire new skills is supported not only by this requirement of fairness but also by reasons of the kind that support the requirement of substantive opportunity, discussed in Chapter 5. The reasons people have to be able to choose careers and develop the skills needed for them do not cease after a person takes his or her first job, but extend through life (whether a person loses that job or not).[28] Third, if one obligation of government in a modern society is to manage the economy in a way that enhances productivity and provides employment for citizens, then it can be a violation of the requirement of equal concern that I discussed in Chapter 2 for a government to fulfill this requirement less fully for workers in the sectors of the economy or regions of the country that lose out as a result of changes in technology and markets than for others. Finding ways to distribute the costs of economic productivity more equitably is of course very difficult.[29] This task is unlikely to be even attempted, however, unless there is effective political will behind it, and this in turn is unlikely to be the case when the political power of unions is weak and economic inequality has the effects on political influence that were discussed in Chapter 6.

The inequality I have been discussing between the incomes of top executives and those of workers is only one aspect of recent increases in inequality. Another is the increase in incomes of those who work in the financial sector. I would address this issue using the normative framework that I have just described. The answer would depend on empirical questions about the need for institutions to raise and allocate capital, the regulation of banks and other financial institutions, and the justifiability of particular financial instruments that I cannot go into here.[30]

I do want to say something, however, about how the framework I have offered applies to the case of inherited wealth, the last source of inequality that I mentioned. Here it is natural to start from the idea that if the assets that a person has accumulated over his or her life were acquired in a way that is legitimate, then that person is entitled to pass these assets on to his or her children, just as he or she is free to spend money in any other way. Stated in this simple form, the claim is too quick, since it simply assumes that a person's entitlement to assets includes the power to transfer them by bequest. But being able to give their children better lives is one of the main reasons people have to work and save. So there are significant liberty-based reasons for allowing them to transfer some assets in this way. Against this, there are reasons for curbing inequality,

---

[28] As Fishkin argues. See *Bottlenecks*, 220ff. and elsewhere.

[29] For some proposals, see Atkinson, *Inequality*, 132 and 237–9.

[30] For an overview, see the Roosevelt Institute report, "Defining Financialization."

in order to limit its undesirable effects. These reasons grow stronger (and, arguably, the reasons for allowing intergenerational transfers grow weaker), not with the size of the total assets transferred, but with the amount that is transferred to any one person.

So the aims of reducing inequality and limiting the concentrated control of capital could be better pursued by taxing recipients of inherited income rather than taxing estates themselves regardless of how they are distributed. There seems no reason why income from gifts and bequests should not be taxed like income from any other source.[31] These taxes, like any others, need to be justified, but the reasons for them would be the same as in the other cases I have discussed, including the need to raise revenue, particularly to fulfill requirements of substantive opportunity and equal concern, and the reasons for limiting inequality in order to curb its undesirable effects.

If the concern is with concentrated control of capital, this would be better served by taxing wealth itself, as Piketty suggests, rather than just its intergenerational transfer.[32] Insofar as this concern is with control of the economy, such a tax could be focused on *capital*, that is to say forms of wealth that involve control over the economy, as opposed to wealth in general, such as ownership of primary residences.[33]

I began this chapter by calling attention to troubling facts about the ratios between incomes of the rich and of the poor, and between the incomes of workers and top managers in large corporations in the U.S. These ratios, and the way they have increased, are troubling. I have argued that the problem does not lie in the ratios themselves, and that the explanation for why they are troubling does not rest on any particular view of what the ratios should be. The problem lies rather with the lack of justification for the factors that give rise to these disparate income levels, and I have tried to spell out how this is so.

Rawls's Difference Principle identifies the question of justice in this same way. It does not specify what the ratios between the expectations of individuals in various social positions must be, but rather specifies the ways in which institutions that generate inequalities in these expectations must be justified. Rawls's principle implies that the inequality in incomes

---

[31] As recommended by Murphy and Nagel. See *The Myth of Ownership*, 159–61.
[32] *Capital in the Twenty-First Century*, chapter 15.
[33] A distinction emphasized by Atkinson, *Inequality*, 95.

that I have described is unjust. But in order to reach this conclusion it is not necessary to accept a principle as strong as Rawls's. The same conclusion follows from the weaker necessary condition I have stated: that in order to be justifiable inequalities must either be unavoidable consequences of the exercise of important personal liberties or result from features of the economic system that are required in order for it to function in a way that benefits all.

The rationale for this weaker claim, however, leads naturally to something very much like Rawls's stronger principle, which requires that justifiable inequalities must not only benefit those who have less but must benefit them as much as possible.[34] An inequality-generating feature of the basic structure could benefit all to some degree—its effects could be a Pareto improvement—even though the resulting distribution of income was quite unfair. Its unfairness, on the view I have offered, would consist in the fact that there are other ways of achieving the same productive advantages while distributing the benefits more equally. These inequality-generating features will thus be "arbitrary" if they have no other justification. So eliminating all inequalities that are arbitrary in the sense I have described will come to something very much like Rawls's Difference Principle. But it is not necessary, in order to condemn existing levels of inequality, to follow the argument through to this conclusion.

How much inequality of income would there be in a society that was not open to the objections I have described? The answer depends on empirical facts about the possibility of alternative ways of organizing the economy. My own guess is that this inequality would not be very great: certainly much less that obtained in the United States in the mid-twentieth century, not to mention what we have seen since that time.

---

[34] "Something very much like" in part because I have allowed considerations of liberty in general (in the two forms I have identified) to count among the reasons for and against features of a basic structure, whereas the primary social goods in terms of which Rawls's Difference Principle is applied include only certain "basic liberties." But this difference is narrowed by the fact that these include important personal liberties such as the right to hold personal property. See Freeman, "Capitalism in the Classical and High Liberal Traditions," 31, and n. 27, and Rawls, *A Theory of Justice*, 53, 54.

10

Conclusions

The view of equality set forth in this book is relational and pluralistic. I have maintained that there are many different reasons for objecting to inequality, and that these depend on the way that an inequality affects or arises from the relations between individuals. In previous chapters I have investigated some of these objections in detail: objections to violations of equal concern (Chapter 2), objections to inequalities in status (Chapter 3), objections to interference with the fairness of economic and political institutions (Chapters 4, 5, and 6), and objections to economic institutions that generate large differences in outcome (Chapter 9). In this final chapter I will state some general conclusions that follow from these analyses.

1. The Plurality of Forms of Inequality

One strength of this pluralistic view is that it recognizes the differences between various forms of inequality. In addition to the inequality between the very rich and the rest of us, there is the inequality between the comfortably well off and the very poor, racial inequality, and the various forms of inequality between men and women. These are all objectionable, but they are objectionable for different reasons, not simply because they are all violations of a single requirement that the prospects of individuals should be equal.

Inequality between the very rich and the rest of society arises from unfair distribution of the benefits and costs of economic productivity, of the kind I discussed in Chapter 9. It also gives rise to unequal access to important means of political influence.

Racial inequality involves objectionable inequality in status, lack of economic opportunity, unequal provision of education and other important public services, and unequal treatment by the legal system.

It also involves a denial of access to effective means of political influence, including in many cases denial of the right to vote. Gender inequality also involves objectionable inequality in status, and lack of equal economic opportunity, because of discrimination in hiring and in access to education, and also because of the unequal distribution of the burdens of family life. It also involves, and has been perpetuated by, discrimination that has prevented women from attaining positions of political influence.

The very poor suffer from lack of economic opportunity, due to lack of access to education, and also suffer from inadequate provision of other important public services such as health care. These problems persist in part because the interests of the poor are inadequately represented in the political system. The poor also suffer from a lack of control over important parts of their lives. They are subject to control by others in their working lives, have little choice of occupation, and suffer from what Jiwei Ci calls agency poverty as well as status poverty.

Although most of the examples of objectionable inequality that I have discussed involve inequality within one country, this does not mean that the view of equality I have set out applies only to cases of this kind, rather than to global inequality. The aim of my inquiry has been to identify the moral basis of different objections to inequality. The different bases of these objections entail differences in the range of cases to which they apply, as can be seen from the following examples.

As I argued in Chapter 1 and Chapter 3, objections based on equal concern presuppose some agent or institution with an obligation to provide certain goods. These are generally national institutions or even more local ones, but the same requirement of equal concern applies to international institutions where they exist. In the case of equality of opportunity, requirements of procedural fairness that have the institutional rationale I describe in Chapter 4 are not limited by national borders. It is as much a violation of procedural fairness to reject better qualified candidates from other countries as it is to pass over local candidates with similar qualifications. But requirements of substantive opportunity, on the other hand, involve obligations to provide education and other conditions for the development of individuals' talents. I have assumed that this obligation falls on local institutions, but it could be argued that it applies more widely. Objections to inequality on the ground of its effects on the fairness of political institutions concern effects on some particular set of such institutions. But this objection can apply worldwide. Large corporations that exist in virtue of the laws of one country can interfere with the fairness of the political process in other countries. Similarly, objections to inequality on the basis of the control it gives some over the lives of others can apply wherever this control exists. Finally, inequality in income and wealth of the kind discussed in Chapter 9, that is objectionable because of the unjustifiability of the institutions that generate it, includes global inequality as well as inequality within one country.

2. Overlapping Objections to Inequality and Egalitarian Priority for the Worst Off

These diverse objections to inequality overlap. Everyone but the very richest has reason to object to features of a basic structure that generate unjustifiable inequality of outcomes. Similarly, all those who suffer from less than equal access to political influence have reason to object to economic inequality that has this effect.

Those who are not provided with an adequate level of important public benefits, such as education, have good reason to object to this. This is in the first instance an objection to insufficiency rather than to inequality, but it becomes an egalitarian objection insofar as the insufficiency results from lack of access to political influence or reflects a violation of equal concern on the part of government. Not only the very poor but those in the middle quintiles as well have objections of these kinds. But the poor have stronger objections, because their level of services is even lower. In addition to these objections, the poor have reason to object to their unequal status, and those who are subject to various forms of discrimination have even stronger reasons of this kind.

The cumulative effect of these overlapping reasons for objecting to inequality is a form of priority for the worst off. The forms of inequality that there is strongest reason to object to, and to eliminate if possible, are the forms affecting the poor, especially those who are both poor and subject to discrimination. But this does not make what I have offered a prioritarian *as opposed to egalitarian* view. This is because most of the reasons supporting this priority, including in particular objections to unequal status, violations of equal concern, and lack of fairness in political and economic institutions, are themselves egalitarian in character. They are egalitarian in at least the wider sense of being objections to the difference between some and others, and in the case of the reasons just mentioned, such as unequal status and violations of equal concern, egalitarian in the narrower sense of being based in the value of particular forms of equality.

3. Giving Equality of Opportunity its Proper Place

It is important not to exaggerate the degree to which equality of opportunity has been achieved. Our economic institutions, including our educational system, continue to embody not only forms of discrimination on racial and other lines but also other forms of procedural unfairness. In addition, we are not close to providing conditions of substantive opportunity for all. It is also important to recognize that equality of opportunity, even if fully realized, would not render the resulting inequalities just. Equality of opportunity *presupposes* some other justification for unequal positions. It could not provide such a justification.

At the same time, however, we should not lose sight of the fact that procedural fairness and substantive opportunity are important, and very much worth pursuing even if they cannot be fully realized. It is therefore important to understand these values properly, and in particular to understand the ideas of ability, merit, effort, and choice in terms of which they are often stated.

4. Avoiding Moralism and Mistaken Ideas of Desert

A proper understanding of the moral significance of ability, effort, and choice enables us to avoid moralism and mistaken ideas of desert. I have tried to provide such an understanding in Chapters 4, 5, and 8. The kind of ability relevant to questions of justice depends on the structure of institutional roles and the developmental conditions that are available in a given society. Ability is therefore not a property of a person, defined independently of any institution, that a just institution should reward. The relevance of choice and effort to the justification of inequalities lies in the fact that individuals' objections to not having certain advantages can be undermined by the fact that they could have had those advantages if they had chosen to make the required effort. But the fact that a person had an opportunity to choose a different outcome can have this legitimating effect only if the person had that opportunity to choose under sufficiently good conditions.

5. Equality and Value

Another theme that emerged in preceding chapters is that whether a society exhibits desirable forms of equality, or objectionable forms of inequality, will depend on the ideas of value prevalent in that society. This dependence figured in several ways in the discussion of status in Chapter 3. Many forms of discrimination involve basic evaluative errors about the importance of certain individual characteristics, such as skin color. Whether being poor involves a lack of status also depends on the evaluative attitudes prevalent in one's society. And the idea that a perfect meritocracy would be a form of objectionable hierarchy depends on the (plausible) assumption that members of such a society would overvalue the kinds of accomplishment that this system rewarded.

This presents a dilemma for our thinking about equality of opportunity. Substantive opportunity requires that individuals grow up in conditions that lead them to see the abilities that would qualify them for positions of advantage as valuable and worth striving for. But a society is open to objection if it encourages individuals to attach excessive importance to these particular forms of accomplishment and success. Achieving an appropriate balance between these is a difficult matter.

6. Economic Inequality and Justifiable Institutions

I agree with Rawls (and with Nozick and Hayek) in holding that there is no valid general principle specifying the pattern that the distribution of income and wealth should take. Whether a distribution of income and wealth is just depends on the nature of the institutions that produce it, and inequalities in income and wealth are fair if the institutions that produce them can be justified in the proper way. The justification of these institutions is a complex matter, depending on empirical facts about the consequences of various economic and political arrangements in a given setting. The task of a work like this is to try to identify the relevant normative elements in such a justification.

My claims about this have been both negative and positive. My negative claims (in Chapters 7 and 8) are that economic institutions cannot be justified by appeal to independent notions of property rights or desert. My positive claim, set out in Chapter 9, is that justification must therefore appeal to the reasons individuals have for accepting such institutions based on how their lives would be affected. Institutions that generate unequal outcomes are not justifiable unless these inequalities could not be avoided without either violating important individual liberties or interfering with the productive process in a way that would make those who have less even worse off. This standard of justifiability is weaker than Rawls's Difference Principle, which holds that inequalities are just only if the institutions that generate them make the worse off as well off as possible. But this weaker principle is strong enough to explain what is objectionable about the levels of inequality prevailing in today's society. And the line of argument leading to this weaker principle lends support to Rawls's stronger version as well.

7. Giving Liberty (for All) its Place

As I have just indicated, the reasons that individuals have for accepting or objecting to institutions include their interests in personal liberty. These include reasons for wanting opportunities to be available, reasons for wanting to be placed in good conditions for choosing among these options, and reasons for objecting to being under the control of others. Justifications for institutions need to take into account reasons of this kind that everyone has, including those against whom rights are enforced as well as holders of those rights.

8. Why does Inequality Matter?

Individuals have many different reasons for objecting to forms of inequality: reasons based on its effects, on the relations with others that it involves, and on the institutions that generate it. These reasons are diverse and do not all derive from any single egalitarian distributive principle. What unifies them is their shared role within the process through which social institutions must be justified to those who are asked to accept them. My view is thus egalitarian at two levels. It is egalitarian at the most abstract level in holding that institutions must be justified to those who are asked to accept them in a way that takes all of their interests seriously and gives them equal weight. It is egalitarian at a more specific level in recognizing the various reasons that individuals have to object to being treated unequally in certain specific ways. These are the reasons why the various forms of inequality matter.

Bibliography

Achen, Christopher H., and Larry M. Bartels, *Democracy for Realists: Why Elections do Not Produce Responsive Government* (Princeton: Princeton University Press, 2016).

Ackerman, Bruce A., and Anne Alstott, *The Stakeholder Society* (New Haven: Yale University Press, 1999).

Allen, Danielle, "Toward a Connected Society," in Earl Lewis and Nancy Cantor (eds), *Our Compelling Interests: The Value of Diversity for Democracy and a Prosperous Society* (Princeton: Princeton University Press, 2016), 71–105.

Anderson, Elizabeth, "What is the Point of Equality?," *Ethics*, 109 (1999), 287–337.

Arneson, Richard, "Equality and Equal Opportunity for Welfare," *Philosophical Studies*, 56.1 (1989), 77–93.

Atkinson, Anthony, *Inequality: What Can Be Done?* (Cambridge, MA: Harvard University Press, 2015).

Bartels, Larry, "Economic Inequality and Political Representation," in Bartels, *Unequal Democracy: The Political Economy of the New Gilded Age* (Princeton: Princeton University Press and Russell Sage Foundation, 2008), 252–82.

Bashir, Omar S., "Testing Inferences about American Politics: A Review of the 'Oligarchy' Result," *Research and Politics*, 2.4 (2016); retrieved from: <http://rap.sagepub.com/content/2/4/2053168015608896>.

Bebchuk, Lucian, and Yaniv Grinstein, "The Growth of Executive Pay," *Oxford Review of Economic Policy*, 21 (2005), 283–303.

Beitz, Charles, *Political Equality* (Princeton: Princeton University Press, 1989).

Bell, Daniel A., *The China Model: Political Meritocracy and the Limits of Democracy* (Princeton: Princeton University Press, 2015).

Bivens, Josh, and Lawrence Mishel, "The Pay of Corporate Executives and Financial Professionals as Evidence of Rents in Top 1 Percent Incomes," *Journal of Economic Perspectives*, 27 (2013), 57–78.

Buchanan, James, "A Hobbesian Interpretation of the Rawlsian Difference Principle," *Kyklos*, 29 (1976), 5–25.

Buchanan, James, "Rules for a Fair Game: Contractarian Notes on Distributive Justice," in *Liberty, Market, and the State: Political Economy in the 1980s* (New York: New York University Press, 1985), 123–39.

Buchanan, James, and Richard A. Musgrave, *Public Finance and Public Choice: Two Contrasting Visions of the State* (Cambridge, MA: MIT Press, 1999).

CDC, *Health Disparities and Inequalities Report—United States* (Washington, D.C.: Center for Disease Control and Prevention, U.S. Department of Health and Human Services, 2013. Retrieved from <cdc.gov>.

Ci, Jiwei, "Agency and Other Stakes of Poverty," *Journal of Political Philosophy*, 21 (2014), 125–50.

Cohen, G. A., "On the Currency of Egalitarian Justice," *Ethics*, 99.4 (1989), 906–44.

Cohen, G. A., "Justice, Freedom, and Market Transactions," in *Self-Ownership, Freedom, and Equality* (Cambridge: Cambridge University Press, 1995), 38–66.

Cohen, G. A., *Self-Ownership, Freedom, and Equality* (Cambridge: Cambridge University Press, 1995).

Cohen, G. A., "Where the Action is: On the Site of Distributive Justice," *Philosophy and Public Affairs*, 26 (1997), 3–30.

Cohen, G. A., *Rescuing Justice and Equality* (Cambridge, MA: Harvard University Press, 2008).

Cohen, G. A., *Why Not Socialism?* (Princeton: Princeton University Press, 2009).

Cohen, Joshua, "Money, Politics, Political Equality," in Cohen, *Philosophy, Politics, Democracy* (Cambridge, MA: Harvard University Press, 2009), 268–302.

Cohen, Joshua, and Charles Sabel, "Extra Rempublicam Nulla Justitia?," *Philosophy and Public Affairs*, 34 (2006), 147–75.

Cottom, M. T., "Why do Poor People 'Waste' Money on Luxury Goods?," Talking Points Memo (2013); retrieved from <http://talkingpointsmemo.com/cafe/why-do-poor-people-waste-money-on-luxury-goods>.

Council of Economic Advisers Policy Brief 2016, "Labor Market Monopsony: Trends, Consequences, and Policy Responses"; retrieved from <https://obamawhitehouse.archives.gov/sites/default/files/page/files/20161025_monopsony_labor_mrkt_cea.pdf>.

Cullen, Mark R., Clint Cummins, and Victor R. Fuchs, "Geographic and Racial Variation in Premature Mortality in the U.S.: Analyzing the Disparities." *PLOS|one*, April 12, 2012; retrieved from <http://journals.plos.org/plosone/article?id=10.1371/journal.pone.0032930>.

Daniels, Norman, "Merit and Meritocracy," *Philosophy and Public Affairs*, 7 (1978), 206–23.

Daniels, Norman, "Fair Equality of Opportunity and Decent Minimums," *Philosophy and Public Affairs*, 14 (1985), 106–10.

Daniels, Norman, *Just Health Care* (New York: Cambridge University Press, 1985).

Deaton, Angus, "What does the Empirical Evidence Tell us about the Injustice of Health Inequalities?," in Nir Eyal, Samia Hurst, Ole Frithof Norheim, and

Daniel Wikler (eds), *Inequalities in Health: Concepts, Measures and Ethics* (Oxford: Oxford University Press, 2013), 263–81.

Dworkin, Ronald, *Taking Rights Seriously* (Cambridge, MA: Harvard University Press, 1978).

Dworkin, Ronald, *Sovereign Virtue: The Theory and Practice of Equality* (Cambridge, MA: Harvard University Press, 2000).

Elster, Jon, *Local Justice: How Institutions Allocate Scarce Goods and Necessary Burdens* (New York: Russell Sage Foundation, 1993).

Enns, Peter K., "Relative Policy Support and Coincidental Representation," *Perspectives on Politics*, 13 (2015), 1053–64.

Enoch, David, Levi Specter, and Talia Fisher, "Statistical Evidence, Sensitivity, and the Legal Value of Knowledge," *Philosophy and Public Affairs*, 40 (2012), 197–224.

Feinberg, Joel, "Justice and Personal Desert," in *Doing and Deserving: Essays in the Theory of Responsibility* (Princeton: Princeton University Press, 1970).

Feinberg, Joel, "Noncomparative Justice," *Philosophical Review*, 83.3 (1974), 297–338.

Fishkin, Joseph, *Bottlenecks* (New York: Oxford University Press, 2014).

Frankfurt, Harry, "Equality as a Moral Ideal," *Ethics*, 98 (1987), 21–43.

Frankfurt, Harry, *On Inequality* (Princeton: Princeton University Press, 2015).

Freeman, Samuel, "Capitalism in the Classical and High Liberal Traditions," *Social Philosophy and Policy*, 28.2 (2011), 19–55.

Fried, Barbara, *The Progressive Assault on Laissez Faire: Robert Hale and the First Law and Economics Movement* (Cambridge, MA: Harvard University Press, 1998).

Friedman, Milton, *Capitalism and Freedom* (Chicago: University of Chicago Press, 1982).

Gaus, Gerald, *Social Philosophy* (Armonk, N.Y.: M. E. Sharp, 1999).

Gaus, Gerald, *The Order of Public Reason* (Cambridge: Cambridge University Press, 2011).

Gauthier, David, *Morals by Agreement* (Oxford: Oxford University Press, 1986).

Gilens, Martin, "Inequality and Democratic Responsiveness," *Public Opinion Quarterly*, 69 (2005), 778–96.

Gilens, Martin, *Affluence and Influence* (Princeton: Princeton University Press, 2012).

Gilens, Martin, "The Insufficiency of 'Democracy by Coincidence': A Response to Peter K. Enns," *Perspectives on Politics*, 13 (2015), 1065–71.

Hacker, Jacob S., "The Institutional Foundations of Middle-Class Democracy," Policy Network; retrieved from <http://www.policy-network.net/pno_detail.aspx?ID=3998>.

Hale, Robert, "Coercion and Distribution in a Supposedly Non-Coercive State," *Political Science Quarterly*, 38 (1923), 470–94.

Hayek, F. A., *The Constitution of Liberty: The Definitive Edition* (Chicago: University of Chicago Press, 1960/2011).

Hayek, F. A., *Studies in Philosophy, Politics, and Economics* (Chicago: University of Chicago Press, 1967).

Julius, A. J., "Nagel's Atlas," *Philosophy and Public Affairs*, 34 (2006), 176–92.

Julius, A. J., "The Possibility of Exchange," *Politics, Philosophy, and Economics*, 12.4 (2013), 361–74.

Kamm, Frances, *Morality, Mortality*, vol. i. *Death and Whom to Save from it* (New York: Oxford University Press, 1993).

Kolodny, Niko, "Rule Over None II: Social Equality and the Justification of Democracy," *Philosophy and Public Affairs*, 42 (2014), 287–336.

Lareau, Annette, *Unequal Childhoods: Class, Race, and Family Life*, 2nd edn (Berkeley: University of California Press, 2011).

Mack, Eric, "The Natural Right of Property," *Social Philosophy and Policy*, 27 (2010), 53–78.

Mankiw, N. Gregory, "Spreading the Wealth around: Reflections Inspired by Joe the Plumber," *Eastern Economic Journal*, 36 (2010), 285–98.

Mankiw, N. Gregory, "Defending the One Percent," *Journal of Economic Perspectives*, 27.3 (2013), 21–34.

Marmot, Michael, *Status Syndrome: How your Social Standing Directly Affects your Health* (London: Bloomsbury, 2004).

Marmot, Michael, G. Rose, M. Shipley, and P. J. Hamilton, "Employment Grade and Coronary Heart Disease in British Civil Servants," *Journal of Epidemiology and Community Health*, 32 (1978) 244–9.

Marx, Karl, *Critique of the Gotha Program*, in *The Marx-Engels Reader*, ed. Robert C. Tucker, 2nd edn (New York: W. W. Norton, 1978).

Meiklejohn, Alexander, *Political Freedom* (New York: Harper & Row, 1965).

Miller, David, *Principles of Social Justice* (Cambridge, MA: Harvard University Press, 1999).

Mishel, Lawrence, and Alyssa Davis, "Top CEOs Make 300 Times More than Typical Workers," Economic Policy Institute Issue Brief, 399; retrieved from <https://www.epi.org/publication/top-ceos-make-300-times-more-than-workers-pay-growth-surpasses-market-gains-and-the-rest-of-the-0-1-percent>.

Murphy, Liam, and Thomas Nagel, *The Myth of Ownership* (New York: Oxford University Press, 2002).

Nagel, Thomas, "The Policy of Preference," in *Mortal Questions* (New York: Cambridge University Press, 1979), 91–105.

Nagel, Thomas, *Equality and Partiality* (Oxford: Oxford University Press, 1991).

Nagel, Thomas, "The Problem of Global Justice," *Philosophy and Public Affairs*, 33 (2005), 113–47.

Nozick, Robert, *Anarchy, State, and Utopia* (New York: Basic Books, 1974).

O'Neill, Martin, "What Should Egalitarians Believe?," *Philosophy and Public Affairs*, 36 (2008), 119–56.

O'Neill, Martin, "The Facts of Inequality," *Journal of Moral Philosophy*, 7 (2010), 397–410.

O'Neill, Martin, and Thad Williamson, "The Promise of Predistribution," *Policy Network*, Sept. 28, 2012; retrieved from <http://www.policy-network.net/pno_detail.aspx?ID=4262&title=The+promise+of+pre-distribution>.

Paine, Thomas, *Agrarian Justice* (written 1795–6); retrieved from: <https://www.ssa.gov/history/paine4.html>.

Parfit, Derek, "Equality or Priority?," in Michael Clayton and Andrew Williams (eds), *The Ideal of Equality* (New York: Palgrave Macmillan, 2000), 81–125.

Peart, Sandra J., and David M. Levy (eds), *The Street Porter and the Philosopher: Conversations on Analytical Egalitariansim* (Ann Arbor: University of Michigan Press, 2008).

Pettit, Philip, *Republicanism: A Theory of Freedom and Government* (Oxford: Oxford University Press, 1999).

Pettit, Philip, *Just Freedom: A Moral Compass for a Complex World* (New York: W. W. Norton, 2014).

Piketty, Thomas, *Capital in the Twenty-First Century* (Cambridge, MA: Harvard University Press, 2014).

Piketty, Thomas, Emmanuel Saez, and Gabriel Zucman, "Distributional and National Accounts: Methods and Estimates for the United States." National Bureau of Economic Research Working Paper, 22945 (2016); retrieved from <http://www.nber.org/papers/w2294>.

Rawls, John, *A Theory of Justice* (Cambridge, MA: Harvard University Press, 1971; 2nd edn, 1991).

Raz, Joseph, *The Morality of Freedom* (New York: Oxford University Press, 1986).

Robertson, James, "The Future of Money: If We Want a Better Game of Life, We'll Have to Change the Scoring System," *Soundings*, 31 (2005), 118–32; retrieved from <http://www.jamesrobertson.com/article/soundings31.pdf>.

Roosevelt Institute, "Defining Financialization"; retrieved from <http://rooseveltinstitute.org/defining-financialization>.

Rousseau, Jean-Jacques, *Discourse on the Origin of Inequality* (Indianapolis: Hackett Publishing Co., 1992).

Saez, Emmanuel, "Striking it Richer: The Evolution of Top Incomes in the United States (Updated with 2014 Preliminary Estimates)"; retrieved from: <https://eml.berkeley.edu/~saez/saez-UStopincomes-2014.pdf>.

Scanlon, T. M., "Freedom of Expression and Categories of Expression," *University of Pittsburgh Law Review*, 40 (1979), 519–50; reprinted in Scanlon, *The Difficulty of Tolerance* (Cambridge: Cambridge University Press, 2003), 84–112.

Scanlon, T. M., "The Significance of Choice," in Sterling M. McMurrin (ed.), *Tanner Lectures in Human Values*, vol. viii (Salt Lake City: University of Utah Press, 1988), 149–216.

Scanlon, T. M., *What we Owe to Each Other* (Cambridge, MA: Harvard University Press, 1998).

Scanlon, T. M., *Moral Dimensions: Permissibility, Meaning, and Blame* (Cambridge, MA: Harvard University Press, 2008).

Scanlon, T. M., "Giving Desert its Due," *Philosophical Explorations*, 16.2 (2013), 101–16.

Scanlon, T. M., "Responsibility and the Value of Choice," *Think*, 12 (2013), 9–16.

Scanlon, T. M., "Forms and Conditions of Responsibility," in Randolph Clarke, Michael McKenna, and Angela M. Smith (eds), *The Nature of Moral Responsibility* (New York: Oxford University Press, 2015), 89–111.

Scheffler, Samuel, "Justice and Desert in Liberal Theory," in *Boundaries and Allegiances* (Oxford: Oxford University Press, 2001), 173–96.

Scheffler, Samuel, "What is Egalitarianism?," *Philosophy and Public Affairs*, 31 (2003), 5–39.

Scheffler, Samuel, "Choice, Circumstance, and the Value of Equality," in *Equality and Tradition* (Oxford: Oxford University Press, 2010), 208–35.

Sen, Amartya, "Just Deserts," *New York Review of Books*, Mar. 4, 1982; retrieved from <http://www.nybooks.com/articles/1982/03/04/just-deserts>.

Sen, Amartya, "The Moral Standing of the Market," *Social Philosophy and Policy*, 2.2 (1985), 1–19.

Sen, Amartya, *Inequality Reexamined* (Cambridge, MA: Harvard University Press, 1992).

Shelby, Tommie, *Dark Ghettos: Injustice, Dissent, and Reform* (Cambridge, MA: Harvard University Press, 2016).

Sher, George, *Equality for Inegalitarians* (Cambridge: Cambridge University Press, 2014).

Skinner, Quentin, *Liberty Before Liberalism* (New York: Cambridge University Press, 1998).

Smith, Adam, *An Inquiry into the Nature of Causes of the Wealth of Nations* (London: Home University, 1910); retrieved from <https://www.washingtonpost.com/news/answer-sheet/wp/2014/12/21/heres-who-got-the-biggest-gates-foundation-education-grants-for-2014>.

Thomson, Judith, "Liability and Individualized Evidence," in Thomson, *Rights, Restitution and Risk*, ed. William Parent (Cambridge, MA: Harvard University Press, 1986), 225–50.

Tomasi, John, *Free Market Fairness* (Princeton: Princeton University Press, 2012).

Van Parjis, Philippe, "Why Surfers Should Be Fed: The Liberal Case for an Unconditional Basic Income," *Philosophy and Public Affairs*, 20 (1991), 101–31.

Van Parjis, Philippe, *Real Freedom for All: What (If Anything) Can Justify Capitalism?* (Oxford: Oxford University Press, 1998).

Westen, Peter, "The Empty Idea of Equality," *Harvard Law Review*, 95.3 (1982), 537–96.

Western, Bruce, and Jake Rosenfeld, "Unions, Norms, and the Rise in U.S. Wage Inequality," *American Sociological Review*, 76 (2011), 513–37.

Wilkinson, Richard, and Kate Pickett, *The Spirit Level: Why More Equal Societies Almost Always Do Better* (London: Penguin/Allen Lane, 2009).

Young, Michael, *The Rise of the Meritocracy* (New Brunswick, NJ: Transaction Publishers, 1994).

Index

interference with requires
justification 95–6
as distinct from power 96–100
objections to control by others 96,
98–102
personal liberties 141, 151, 151*n34*, 157
life expectancy
and economic inequality 13
international disparities in 11–12
and equal concern 12–14
Lindsay, John 87
lotteries 44, 50, 70
luck egalitarianism 9, 9*n10*, 63*n21*

Mack, Eric 105*n12*
Malawi, life expectancy in 11–12, 12–13
Mankiw, N. Gregory 38*n18*, 117, 119,
124, 128–9, 140
Marmot, Michael 2*n2*, 6*n6*
Marx, Karl 141*n14*
Meiklejohn, Alexander 92*n21*
merit *see* ability
meritocracy 33–6, 45*n2*, 156
vs. democracy 77, 79
and procedural fairness 44–5
Miller, David 125*n9*
Mishel, Lawrence 37*n17*, 134, 143–4
monopolisation 146*n25*
of the media 90–1
moral equality, basic 4
moralism 60, 61, 63, 72–3, 155–6
Murphy, Liam 103–4*nn9–11*, 107*n14*,
150*n31*
Musgrave, Richard 55*n7*

Nagel, Thomas 9–10, 32, 35, 69*n30*,
103–4*nn9–11*, 107*n14*, 150*n31*
nepotism 43, 49, 50
New Jersey
school funding 15, 87, 89
reapportionment 87, 88*n18*
Nozick, Robert 1–2, 3, 4, 14, 21,
53*n1*, 95, 96, 105*n12*, 108*nn15–16*,
110, 112, 114*n19*, 129*n15*, 140,
141*n13*, 156

O'Neill, Martin 2*n2*, 3*n3*, 102*n8*
Original Position 47*n6*, 137

Paine, Thomas 55*n5*
Parfit, Derek 3*n3*, 9*n10*

Peart, Sandra J. 55*n7*
Pettit, Philip 98*n6*, 99*n7*
Pickett, Kate 2*n2*
Piketty, Thomas 38*n19*, 117, 128*n14*,
133, 135, 138*n9*, 143, 144, 146*n23*,
147*n26*, 150
Plato 92
political liberties, value of 89–92
political fairness 6, 74–94
and economic inequality 74–5,
81–2, 93
and equal opportunity for
influence 88
vs. equality of economic
opportunity 78–9
poverty
and prioritarianism 3
and status 29–32
'stakes' of 30
as threat to substantive opportunity
power
distinguished from liberty 98
inequality as source of 2, 94, 152
predistribution 102, 104, 104*n11*, 139
prioritarianism 3, 154
procedural fairness 40–52, 53, 66
and discrimination 43–4
as distinct from substantive
opportunity 76
and efficiency 51
and ability in the institution-
dependent sense 44–5
need for due consideration 52
violations of 67–8
property rights 103, 105–6, 106–16
institutionally defined 107
intellectual property 102, 109–10
justification of 108–10

racial inequality 4, 152–3
see also discrimination
Rawls, John 27, 30, 35–6, 39, 41–2, 46–7,
54, 55, 56, 135–7, 136, 142, 151, 156
on moral arbitrariness 46
on openness 57, 57*n11*
on political fairness 82
on value of liberties 79
on welfare state capitalism 75
on willingness 62, 65
see also Difference Principle; Fair
Equality of Opportunity